Of Mistresses, Tigresses and Other Conquests

GIACOMO CASANOVA

Of Mistresses, Tigresses and Other Conquests

Translated by STEPHEN SARTARELLI *and* SOPHIE HAWKES

GREAT 🐧🐧 LOVES

PENGUIN BOOKS

Published by the Penguin Group
Penguin Books Ltd, 80 Strand, London WC2R 0RL, England
Penguin Group (USA) Inc., 375 Hudson Street, New York, New York 10014, USA
Penguin Group (Canada), 90 Eglinton Avenue East, Suite 700, Toronto, Ontario, Canada M4P 2Y3
(a division of Pearson Penguin Canada Inc.)
Penguin Ireland, 25 St Stephen's Green, Dublin 2, Ireland
(a division of Penguin Books Ltd)
Penguin Group (Australia), 250 Camberwell Road, Camberwell, Victoria 3124, Australia
(a division of Pearson Australia Group Pty Ltd)
Penguin Books India Pvt Ltd, 11 Community Centre, Panchsheel Park, New Delhi – 110 017, India
Penguin Group (NZ), 67 Apollo Drive, Rosedale, North Shore 0632, New Zealand
(a division of Pearson New Zealand Ltd)
Penguin Books (South Africa) (Pty) Ltd, 24 Sturdee Avenue,
Rosebank, Johannesburg 2196, South Africa

Penguin Books Ltd, Registered Offices: 80 Strand, London WC2R 0RL, England

www.penguin.com

This translation first published in the United States of America by
Marsilio Publishers Corp. 2000
This translation first published in Great Britain in Penguin Classics 2005
This extract published in Penguin Books 2007

1

Typeset by Rowland Phototypesetting Ltd, Bury St Edmunds, Suffolk
Printed in England by Clays Ltd, St Ives plc

978-0-141-03279-5

Contents

Giacomo Casanova (1725–1798) was one of the most colourful figures of the eighteenth century. He was a writer, adventurer, soldier, free thinker, con man, gambler, gourmand, violinist, lottery director and spy, and consorted with many notable figures of his day. In the course of his many occupations, he also vigorously pursued the amatory adventures that made his reputation as a legendary seducer. He wrote several novels as well as journalism and poetry, translated Homer's *Iliad* into Italian, and is said to have contributed to the libretto of Mozart's *Don Giovanni*. He began to write his memoirs in 1791. At 3,600 manuscript pages, his *Histoire de ma vie*, from which these extracts are taken, remained unfinished at the time of his death in 1798.

The Freedom of Man

I begin by informing my reader that for everything good or bad that I have done throughout my life, I am certain I have always earned due approbation or reproof, and must therefore consider myself a free man. The doctrine of the Stoics and all similar sects regarding the power of Destiny is a figment of the imagination deriving from atheism. I myself am not only monotheistic but Christian, and fortified by philosophy, which has never done any harm.

I believe in the existence of an immortal GOD, creator and master of all forms. What assures me that I have never doubted Him is that I have always counted on His providence, turning to Him through the medium of prayer in all my moments of distress, and finding my entreaties always answered. Despair kills; prayer dispels it. After praying, man gains confidence and acts. Knowing by what means the Being of Beings wards off the misfortune that threatens those who seek his intercession is something beyond man's understanding. The moment we contemplate the incomprehensibility of divine providence, we find ourselves compelled to adore Him. Our ignorance becomes our sole resource, and only those who cherish it are truly happy. We must therefore pray to GOD and believe we have received grace even when appearances tell us that we have not. As for the position the body must assume when addressing our wishes to the Creator, this is indicated in a line of Petrarch:

> *Con le ginocchia della mente inchine.*
> ('With the knees of the mind bent.')

Man is free; but not unless he believes he is, for the more power he attributes to Destiny, the more he deprives himself of that power which GOD gave him when He granted him *reason*.

Reason is but a fragment of the Creator's divinity. If we use it to make ourselves humble and just, we cannot help but please Him whose gift it was to us. GOD only ceases to be GOD for those who conceive his non-existence as possible. They could not suffer any greater punishment than this.

Though man is free, he must not believe that he is free to do whatever he wants. He becomes a slave when he resolves to act upon a passion that stirs him. *Nisi paret imperat.* ('If he does not obey, he commands.') He who has the strength to take no further steps until calm prevails is a wise man. Such a being is rare.

The thoughtful reader will note that as I had no single aim in writing these memoirs, the only system I had, if it can be called such, was to let myself go whither the wind that was blowing would take me. What vicissitudes in this freedom from method! My misfortunes as well as my fortunes have proved to me that in the physical as well as spiritual worlds, good comes from bad, as bad from good. My strayings will either point thoughtful people to the opposite paths, or teach them the great art of riding along the edge of the precipice without falling in. One need only have courage, for strength without confidence is useless. I have often seen good fortune befall me as the result of a reckless act that should rather have led me into the abyss; and, even while scolding myself, I have given thanks to GOD for this. I have also seen, quite to the contrary, overwhelming misfortune arise from conduct tempered by wisdom. And this has humbled me; but, certain of having been right, I easily got over it.

Despite an excellent moral foundation, the inevitable fruit of the divine principles rooted in my heart, I was prey to my senses throughout my life. I took pleasure in straying, and I lived perpetually in error, with no other consolation than an awareness of doing so. For this reason I hope, dear reader, that far from finding my story impudent and boastful in character, you will find it written in a spirit best suited to a general confession, even though in the style of my narratives you will find neither the tone of a penitent nor the restraint of someone blushing while recounting his escapades. They are follies of youth. I now laugh at them, as you will see, and if you are kind, you will laugh along with me.

You will laugh when you learn that I thought nothing of deceiving idiots, scoundrels and fools when I needed to do so. As for my deceptions of women, these are not of the sort to be tallied, since when love has a hand in things, each party usually dupes the other. Fools, however, are another matter entirely. I always take great delight in remembering those I have lured into my traps, for fools are insolent and their presumptions insult the mind. Thus we avenge intelligence when we deceive a fool, and the victory is worth the trouble, for he is protected as if with armor, and we do not know where to strike him. Deceiving a fool, in short, is an endeavor worthy of a man of wit. What has instilled in me, since my birth, an invincible hatred of this breed, is that I feel like a fool whenever I find myself in their company. We must, however, distinguish them from those we call stupid, for indeed I am rather fond of such men, who are stupid only for want of proper breeding. I have found some to be quite upright, in fact, and who in the nature of their stupidity had a kind of intelligence. They are like eyes that, if not for their cataracts, would be very beautiful.

If, dear reader, you examine this preface well, you will easily guess its purpose. I have written it because I want you to know me before you read me. Only in coffee-houses and inns do we converse with strangers.

I have written my history, and surely no one could take exception to it. Still, am I wise to present it to a public I know only in the worst light? No. I know it is foolish. But since I need to keep myself busy and to laugh, why should I refrain from committing such a folly?

Expulit elleboro morbum, bilemque meraco.
('He chased away illness and bile with hellebore.')

An Ancient tells me, with a teacher's tone: *If you have not done things worthy of being written about, at least write things worthy of being read.* It is a precept as beautiful as a diamond of the first water cut in England, but it is of no use to me, since I am writing neither the story of a famous man nor a novel. Worthy or unworthy as it may be, my life is my subject, and my subject is my life. Having lived it without ever imagining I would wish one day to write it down, it is perhaps of greater interest than it would have been had I lived it with the intention of writing about it in my old age and, what is more, publishing it.

In this year of 1797, at the age of seventy-two, when I can say *vixi* ('I lived') even though I still breathe, I can think of no greater amusement than to entertain myself with my own adventures and give dignified cause for laughter to the good company listening to me, who have always shown me friendship and whose society I have always frequented. To write well, I need only imagine that they will read me: *Quaecumque dixi, si placuerint, dictavit auditor.* ('If what I say pleases the listener, let him say so.') As for the uninitiated, whom I am powerless to prevent reading my story, I am content to know that it was not for them that I wrote it.

In recalling the pleasures I enjoyed, I relive them, while I laugh at the pains I endured and no longer feel. A member of the universe, I speak to the air, and fancy myself giving an account of my conduct of affairs the way a major-domo does to his master before retiring. As for my future, I have never, as a philosopher, cared to worry much about it, since I can know nothing about it; as a Christian, I know faith must believe without reason, and the purest faith maintains a deep silence. I know I have existed and, being certain of this precisely because I have felt, I also know that I shall no longer exist when I have ceased to feel. If I do happen still to feel after my death, I shall no longer doubt anything; but I will give the lie to all those who come and tell me I am dead.

As my story must begin with the most remote event my memory can recollect, it will begin when I was eight years and four months of age. Before this time, if it is true that *vivere cogitare est* ('to live is to think'), I did not live: I vegetated. Since human thought consists only in comparisons made in order to examine relationships, it cannot precede the existence of memory. The organ most characteristic of man did not develop in my head until eight years and four months after my birth; only at that moment did my soul begin to be susceptible to impressions. How an immaterial substance that can *nec tangere nec tangi* ('neither touch nor be touched') is able to receive impressions, no man has ever been able to explain.

One consolatory philosophy claims, in accordance with religion, that the soul's dependence on the senses and organs is purely fortuitous and transitory, and that it will be free and happy when the death of the body liberates it from their tyrannical power. That's all very beautiful but, religion aside, it is hardly certain. As I therefore could never be absolutely sure of my immortality before ceasing to exist, you will forgive me if I was in no hurry to discover this truth. A knowledge paid for with life is paid too dearly. While waiting,

I shall worship God, avoiding all unjust action and shunning unjust men, without, however, doing them harm. It is enough that I abstain from doing them good. One must not feed snakes.

I must also say something about my temperament and character. Those of my readers who indulge me in this regard will prove not without their share of decency and intelligence.

I have had all four of the temperaments: the phlegmatic in childhood, the sanguine in youth, then the choleric, and lastly the melancholic, which it appears will be my lot till the end. Conforming my diet to my constitution, I have always enjoyed good health; and having learnt that what spoils health is always an excess of either food or abstinence, I have always been my own doctor. All the same, I have found abstinence far more dangerous. Excess causes indigestion; but dearth causes death. Today, old as I am, I need to eat only once a day, despite the excellent condition of my stomach. What makes up for this privation is the sweet sleep I enjoy and the ease with which I set my thoughts down on paper without needing to resort to paradox or to coil sophistry around sophistry, which would only fool me more than my readers, since I could never bring myself to give them false coin if I knew it to be false.

My sanguine temperament made me very sensitive to the allurements of all forms of sensual delight; I was always cheerful and eager to move on from one pleasure to the next, and ingeniously inventing new forms of it. From this derived my inclination to seek new friendships, as well as my ease in breaking them off, although it was always in full knowledge of the reasons, and never out of fickleness. Defects of temperament cannot be corrected, since temperament is beyond our powers. Character, however, is another matter. The heart and mind are its constituent elements, with temperament having very little influence on it. It thus follows that character depends on upbringing, and can be corrected and reformed.

I leave it to others to decide whether my own is good or bad; but such as it is, it can be easily seen in my physiognomy by those experienced in such matters. Only there, in the face, is a man's character in plain view, for that is its seat. We note that men who have no physiognomy, and there are many, likewise have nothing of what we might call character. And thus, the diversity of physiognomies will be found equal to the diversity of characters.

Having recognized that my entire life I have acted more on the basis of sentiment than reflection, I have concluded that my conduct depended more on my character than on my intellect, after a long war between the two, in which I alternately found myself possessed of too little intellect for my character, and too little character for my intellect.

But let us forget all that, since it is true that *si brevis esse volo obscurus fio*. ('When I want to be brief, I become obscure.')

I believe that without offense to modesty, I may appropriate these words from my beloved Virgil:

Nec sum adeo informis: nuper me in litore vidi
Cum placidum ventis staret mare.

('I am not so ugly; I just saw myself in the water, when the sea was calm.')

Cultivating the pleasures of the senses was my principle concern throughout my life; none, indeed, was ever more important to me. Feeling as though I was born for the fair sex, I have always loved it and let it love me as much as I could. I have also passionately loved good food and all things made to arouse curiosity.

I have had friends who treated me well, and I was quite pleased to have always been able to give them tokens of my gratitude. I have also had detestable enemies who persecuted me and whom I did not destroy because I was unable. I would never have forgiven them had I not forgotten the harm they did me. A man who forgets a wrong has not forgiven it; for forgiveness derives from a heroic sentiment in a noble heart and generous spirit, whereas forgetting is the product of a feeble memory or the sweet nonchalance that is friend to the gentle soul, or of the need for calm and peace. For hatred, in the end, kills the wretch who is pleased to feed it.

Those who call me sensual are wrong, for the power of my senses has never torn me away from my duties, when I have had any. For the same reason, one should never have called Homer a drunkard: *Laudibus arguitur vini vinosus Homerus*. ('Homer's praise of wine proves his love of it.')

I have always loved highly savory dishes, such as macaroni made by a good Neapolitan cook, *olla podrida*, the glutinous codfish of Newfoundland, aromatic game meats, and cheeses that attain perfection when the tiny creatures inhabiting them begin to become visible. As for women, I have always found that the one I loved smelled good, and the stronger her perspiration, the sweeter she smelled to me.

What depraved tastes! And how shameful to acknowledge them without blushing! This reproach tickles me to laughter. Thanks to my coarse tastes, I am so shameless as to believe myself happier than the rest, first of all because I think my tastes make me more sensitive to pleasure. Happy are those who can find it without harm to anyone; mad are those who think the Supreme Being could ever enjoy the sorrow, pain and abstinence they offer up to Him in sacrifice, and that He cherishes only the fanatics who seek out such suffering. GOD could never demand of his creatures anything more than that they practice the virtues whose germ he planted in their souls, and He never gave us anything except for the purpose of making us happy: pride, aspiration to praise, emulation, strength, courage and a power that no tyranny can take away from us: that of killing ourselves when, after correct or incorrect estimation, we have the misfortune of finding it to our advantage. This is the greatest proof of our moral freedom, which the Sophists so strongly denied. It is, however, rightly abhorred by nature, and thus all religions must forbid it.

A supposed freethinker once told me I could not call

myself a philosopher if I admitted the existence of revelation.

If we do not doubt it in science, why not admit it in matters of religion? It is only a question of form. The spirit speaks to the spirit, and not to the ears. The principles of everything we know can only have been revealed to those who communicated them to us through the great and supreme principle that contains them all. The bee building its hive, the swallow making its nest, the ant digging its burrow, the spider weaving its web, would never have made anything without some prior, timeless revelation. We must either believe that this is so, or admit that matter can think. Why not, as Locke would say, if GOD wished it so? But we do not dare do such honor to matter. Let us therefore be content with revelation.

The great philosopher who believed, after studying nature, that he could claim victory by recognizing GOD in it, died too soon. Had he lived a little while longer, he would have gone much further, and would not have had far to go. Finding himself in his maker, he could no longer have denied Him: *in eo movemur, et sumus*. ('We move and are in Him.') He would have found Him inconceivable; but this would not have troubled him. Could GOD, the supreme principle of all principles, who has no principle, ever conceive Himself, if in order to conceive himself he needed to know his own principle? O blissful ignorance! Spinoza, the virtuous Spinoza, died before achieving such ignorance. He would have died a wise man, with a right to expect reward for his virtues, had he assumed his soul to be immortal.

It is not true that it is unbefitting to true virtue to expect reward, and that this compromises its purity. Quite to the contrary, expectation serves to sustain virtue, since man is too weak to want to be virtuous only to please himself. I consider the story of Amphiaraus, who *vir bonus esse quam videri malebat* ('preferred to be rather than to seem a good man'), to be mere fable. In short, I believe there is no honest man in the world who does not have some sort of expectation; and I shall tell you now of my own.

I expect friendship, esteem and gratitude from my readers. Gratitude, if they can learn from these memoirs and take pleasure in them. Esteem, if, in judging me fairly, they find me possessed of more virtues than faults. And friendship, once they find me worthy thereof, for the frankness and good faith with which I abandon myself, without disguise, and such as I am, to their judgment.

They will find that I have always loved the truth with such passion that I often began by lying to force the truth into certain heads unfamiliar with its charms. They will not condemn me when they see me empty my friends' purses in order to indulge my whims; for these same friends entertained vain fantasies, and by giving them hope of success in them, I was attempting to cure them of their folly by disabusing them of their illusions. I would deceive them so that they might become wiser; and I did not believe myself blameworthy, for it was not greed that made me act. To pay for my pleasures, I used money intended to obtain things impossible to possess in nature. I would think myself blameworthy if today I were rich. But I have nothing; I have thrown everything away, and that is my consolation and justification. That money was intended for mad schemes; I diverted its use to my own follies.

If I were mistaken in my desire to please, I admit I would be saddened, but not so much as to regret having written these memoirs, for nothing could prevent me from having amused myself. Cruel boredom! Only by oversight could the authors of Hell's punishments have forgotten to include it among them.

I confess, however, that I cannot help but fear the disapproval of my audience. So natural is this fear, I dare not claim to be above it; and far be it from me to seek consolation in the hope that when these memoirs finally appear I shall no longer be alive. I cannot without horror imagine myself incurring some obligation with death, which I detest. Whether happy or unhappy, life is the only treasure man possesses, and those who do not love it are unworthy of it. One may prefer honor to life, but only because infamy spoils it. And if, when forced to choose, one kills oneself, philosophy must keep silent. O death! Cruel law of nature that man's reason can only reject, since you are made only to destroy it! Cicero says that death delivers us from our suffering. But the great philosopher notes only the expenditure, and does not tally the receipts. I do not remember whether, when he was writing his *Tusculanae*, his Tulliola was already dead. Death is a monster that chases the rapt spectator from the theater before the play he is watching with infinite interest has ended. This alone is reason enough to despise it.

You will not find all my adventures in these memoirs. I have omitted those that might offend the people whose part in them would have cast them in an unpleasant light. In spite of this, some will surely find me at times too indiscreet, and I am sorry for this. Should I attain wisdom before I die, and there is still time, I shall burn everything. I haven't the strength to do it now.

Those who find I paint my love affairs in too much detail will be wrong to think so, unless they believe I am not a good painter. I beg their forgiveness all the same, if my old soul is so reduced as to find joy only in reminiscence. The virtuous will skip all those scenes that might alarm them, I am pleased to advise in this preface. So much the worse for those who do not read it. (. . .)

I have written these memoirs not for the young, who to keep from falling must spend their early years in ignorance, but for those who, having lived too much, have become immune to seduction and who, from having lived too long in the fire, have become Salamanders. As true virtues are merely habits, I dare say that the truly virtuous are those fortunate people who practice virtue without any effort at all. They haven't the slightest notion of intolerance. And it is for them that I have written my story. I have written it in French, and not Italian, because the French language is more widely spoken than my own. Purists will, no doubt, find native turns of phrase in my style, and they will be right to criticize me if this prevents my being clearly understood. The Greeks enjoyed

Theophrastus, despite his Eresian phrasing and the Romans Titus Livy, despite his *patavinity*. If I prove interesting to my readers, I might, I think, aspire to the same indulgence. Indeed, all of Italy enjoys Algarotti, even though his style is fraught with gallicisms.

It is, however, worth noting that of all the living languages that have a place in the Republic of Letters, French is the only one that was forbidden by its presiding judges to enrich itself at the expense of other tongues, while the others, all richer than the French, pillaged it of its words as well as its manners as soon as they discovered they could embellish themselves with these petty thefts. Yet those who subjected it to this law had agreed upon its poverty. They said that as it had attained all the beauties of which it was capable, the slightest foreign element would disfigure it. Such a sentence may have been the fruit of prejudice. The entire nation, at the time of Lulli, passed the same judgement on its music, until Rameau came along to disabuse them. At present, under the Republican government, the eloquent orators and learned writers have already convinced all of Europe that they will soon raise the tongue to a height of beauty and power such as the world has never before seen in a language. In the space of five short years it has already gained some hundred new words astonishing for their sweetness, majesty, and harmony. What more beautiful could one invent in matters of language than *ambulance, franciade, monarchien, and sansculottisme*? Vive la République. It is impossible for a body without a head to commit follies.

The banner I have hoisted will explain my digressions and the commentaries I make, perhaps too often, on my exploits of every sort: *nequicquam sapit qui sibi non sapit*. ('He knows nothing who does not profit from what he knows.') For the same reason I have always needed to hear myself praised in good company:

> *Excitat auditor studium, laudataque virtus*
> *crescit, et immensum gloria calcar habet.*

('The audience spurs the effort, the praise increases the skill, and glory is a powerful stimulant.')

I should have gladly displayed the proud axiom: *Nemo leditur nisi a seipso*, ('One always crafts one's own unhappiness.') had I not feared shocking the vast number of people who, when anything goes wrong for them, cry: *It's not my fault*. One must leave them that small consolation, otherwise they would hate themselves; and from such hatred spring the plans to kill oneself.

As for me, I have always known myself to be the principal cause of all of the misfortunes that have befallen me. Thus I took pleasure in finding myself able to be my own pupil and compelled to love my teacher.

A Spy in the House of Love

Here I was in the capital of Austria for the first time, at the fine age of twenty-eight. I had a few possessions but hardly any money; I was forced to bide my time until a letter of exchange from Signor Bragadin was returned to me, at which time I drew upon it at once. The only other letter I had was from the poet Migliavacca of Dresden, recommending me to the illustrious abbé Metastasio, whose acquaintance I was most anxious to make. I presented it to him two days later, and in an hour's conversation I found him grander than his works had foretold in matters of erudition, and modest in a manner I found unnatural at first. I very quickly perceived, however, that his modesty was genuine, when it disappeared the moment he recited something of his own composition, whose beauties he pointed out himself. I mentioned his tutor Gravina to him, and he recited five or six unpublished stanzas he had composed upon his death. I saw him shed tears, moved by the sweetness of his own poetry. After reciting them, he added these words:

'*Ditemi il vero: si può dir meglio?*' ('Tell me the truth, can one say it better?')

I answered that he alone had the right to think it impossible.

I asked him if his beautiful verse cost him much

effort to write, and he promptly showed me four or five pages he had covered with corrections in his desire to reduce fourteen lines to perfection. He assured me that he had never been able to write more than this in one day. This confirmed a truth I already knew, that the lines most difficult for a poet to write are those which uninitiated readers think were written effortlessly. I asked him which of his operas he liked best, and he said *Attilio Regolo*, adding:

'*Ma questo non vuol già dire che sia il migliore.*' ('But that does not mean it is the best.')

I told him that all his works had been translated into French prose and that the publisher had gone bankrupt, for it was impossible to read them, and that this showed the power and beauty of his poetry. He replied that another fool in the last century had ruined himself by translating Ariosto into French prose; and he had a good laugh at the expense of those who maintained, and who continue to maintain, that a work in prose can ever rightly be called a poem. As for his ariettas, he told me that he had never written one without setting it to music himself, but that ordinarily he showed his music to no one. He laughed heartily at those Frenchmen who thought that it was possible to adapt words to music composed in advance. He made a very philosophical comparison:

'It is,' he said, 'as if you said to a sculptor: here is a bit of marble, make me a Venus and show me her face before you have developed her features.'

At the Imperial Library I was greatly surprised to find M. de la Haye with two Poles and a young

Venetian gentleman, whom his father had put at his side to give him a good education. I embraced him several times. I had thought he was in Poland. He told me he was in Vienna on business and would be back in Venice in the summer. We visited each other in turn, and when I told him I had no money, he immediately lent me fifty sequins, for which I was most grateful. He told me his friend the baron of Bavois was already a lieutenant-colonel in the Venetian service, and this news pleased me immensely. Bavois had had the good luck to be chosen as adjutant-general by Signor Morosini, whom the Republic had made commissioner of borders upon his return from the embassy in France. I was delighted at the good fortune of anyone who must recognize me as its principle cause. In Vienna I also learned beyond any doubt that M. de la Haye had been a Jesuit; but I dared not mention it to him.

Not knowing where to go, and wanting to amuse myself, I went to a rehearsal of the opera that was to open after Easter, and there I found Bodin, the *Primo ballerino*, who had married La Geoffroi. I had seen them both in Turin. There I also found Campioni, husband of the beautiful Ancilla, who told me he had divorced her because she dishonored him. Campioni was a great dancer, and a great gambler. I took up residence with him.

Everything in Vienna was beautiful; there was great wealth and great luxury. But life was very difficult for the devotees of Venus. Wretched spies, called *commissioners of chastity*, implacably tormented all the pretty girls. The empress, who possessed all the other virtues, lacked that of tolerance when it came to illicit love between a man and a woman. This great and very religious sovereign hated mortal sin in general, and wished to attain merit before God by extirpating it; she thus rightly believed that it must be persecuted with meticulous care. And so she took into her royal hands the register of what we call the deadly sins, found that there are seven, and thought she could overlook six; but lechery seemed unforgivable to her, and it was against this sin that all her zeal unleashed itself.

'It is possible,' she said, 'not to recognize pride, for it hides behind the banner of dignity. Avarice is atrocious, but we must be careful, for it may look like thrift to those who love money. As for anger, it is an illness whose fits are murderous, but homicide is punished by death. Gluttony may be nothing more than a love of good food, which passes for a virtue in polite society, and is related to appetite. So much the worse for those who die of indigestion. Envy is never openly admitted, and sloth is punished by boredom. But what I cannot tolerate is lust. My subjects are free to admire all the women they find pretty, and women will do anything they can to seem so; people may desire one another as much as they please, I cannot stop them. But I will never suffer the unworthy act that aims to satisfy this desire, though it be inseparable from human nature and the cause of the propagation of the species. Let them marry, if they want to taste these pleasures, and may all those who want to procure them with money die, and may all the wretched women, whose lives depend on what they hope to gain by their charms, be sent to Temisvar. I know Rome is indulgent on this matter, in order, they say, to prevent sodomy, incest and adultery. But my climate is different; my Germans are not quite so bedeviled as the Italians, who do not have, as they do here, the bottle to fall back on. All debauchery of significance will be closely watched as well, and when I find that a woman is unfaithful to her husband, I will lock her up too, notwithstanding the claim that her husband is her only master. This argument cannot hold in my lands, for husbands are too mild here. Fanatical husbands who claim that by punishing their wives I am dishonoring them may shout all they want. Are they not already dishonored?'

'But madame, dishonor can only come from public knowledge, and besides, you could be mistaken.'

'Be quiet.'

From this cruel way of thinking, fruit of the sole defect that the great Maria Theresa had *sub specie recti* ('under the guise of rectitude') arose all the injustices and depredations committed by the brutes known as commissioners of chastity. These men seized and imprisoned, at all hours of the day and night, every young woman they found walking alone in the streets of Vienna, though she might be on her way to earn her bread, even honestly. But how would anyone know if these women were going to someone's house for comfort, or if they were looking for someone to give them comfort? A spy would follow them at a distance; the police had five hundred in their pay and they did not wear uniforms. When a woman entered a house, the spy who had observed her, unable to see to what floor she had gone, would wait for her below, seize her and demand to know whom she had been visiting and what she had been doing, and if there were the least hint of uncertainty in her answers, her tormentor would take her to prison, first seizing everything she had in the way of money or jewelry, which was never seen again. Once at Leopoldstadt, in a scene of confusion, a girl who was fleeing, whom I did not know, slipped a gold watch into my hands, which she was afraid would become the spoils of those who wanted to take her to the Stockhaus. A month later I returned it to her, after she told me her story and by what sacrifices she was delivered from her ordeal. All the women who walked in the streets of Vienna were reduced to the ruse of carrying a rosary in their hands. In this way they avoided summary arrest, for they would say that they were going to church, and Maria Theresa would have hung any commissioner for interfering with them. So oppressed was Vienna by these rogues, a man who needed to pass water had to be careful to find a place where no one could see him. I was very surprised one day to find myself interrupted by a brute in a round wig, who threatened me with arrest if I did not go somewhere else.

'Why, if you please?'

'Because on your left there is a woman at the window who can see you.'

I looked, and indeed I saw the figure of a woman at a fifth-floor window who, had she had an opera glass, could have determined whether I was Jewish or Christian. I obeyed with a laugh, and told the story to everyone; but nobody found it unusual.

I went to the *Écrevisse* to dine with Campioni at a table d'hôte and was surprised to see Bepe il Cadetto there, whom I had known at the time of my arrest in the Spanish army, then seen again at Venice, and later in Lyons under the name of Don Giuseppe Marcati. Campioni, who had been his associate in Lyons, embraced him, spoke to him privately, and told me before we sat down that the gentleman had once again assumed his true name, and that he was Count d'Afflisio. He told me that after dinner they would put together a bank of faro, in which I would hold a small interest, and for this reason I should abstain from playing. I went along with the idea. We made the bank, Afflisio won, Captain Beccaria threw his cards in his face; but the prudent Afflisio paid no attention. We all went to the café, Afflisio, Campioni and I, with a handsome officer who looked at me and smiled, but in a manner which did not offend good manners.

'I'm smiling because you do not recognize me.'

'No, sir, but you do look familiar.'

'Nine years ago I led you to the Rimini gate on the order of Prince Lobkowitz.'

'You are Baron Weiss.'

'Precisely.'

He offered me his friendship and promised to provide me in Vienna with every pleasure within his power. Indeed that evening he presented me at the home of a countess, where I met the abbé Testagrossa, known as 'Bighead,' who was the duke of Modena's minister and well-respected at court, for it was he who had negotiated the marriage between the Archduke and Beatrice d'Este. In this company I met the count of Roggendorf and a Count Sarotin, as well as several Fräuleins and a baroness who had seen better days but was still attractive. We dined, and they called me Baron. It did no good to tell them I had no title; they answered that I had to be something in their society and I could not be less than a baron and therefore I should agree to be one if I wanted to be received anywhere in Vienna. So I consented. The baroness's airy manner gave me to understand that I was to her taste, and that she would accept my courtship; I paid her a visit the next day. She told me to come in the evening if I liked gaming, and I met several players, including Tramontini, whose wife I already knew as Signora Tesi. In this house I also met three or four Fräuleins, who, undaunted by the commissioners of chastity, were devoted to love and so magnanimous that they did not fear compromising their nobility by accepting money. After discovering the privileges these young ladies enjoyed, I realized that the commissioners of chastity only bothered those who did not frequent prominent houses.

The baroness told me that I could present my friends to her, if I had any, and after consulting with Campioni I brought Afflisio, Baron Weiss and even Campioni who, as a dancer, had no need of a title. Afflisio played, held the bank, won, and Tramontini introduced him to his wife, who introduced him to her prince of Sachsen-Hildburghausen. It was in Vienna that Afflisio made his great fortune, before coming to a bad end twenty-five years later. Tramontini, after becoming his associate in the great gambling parties he organized at Afflisio's urging, easily arranged for his wife to have the duke immediately accord Afflisio the rank of captain in the service of Their Imperial and Royal Austrian Majesties. It did not take long, for three weeks later I saw him in uniform; and by the time I left Vienna, he was already in possession of a hundred thousand florins. The empress loved to play games of chance, as did the emperor, but not to punt. He would have someone hold the bank. He was a good ruler, magnificent yet thrifty. I once saw him in imperial regalia and was surprised to find him dressed in the Spanish manner. He seemed to me the image of Charles v, who had instituted this fashion, which still persisted even though no emperor after him was Spanish, and Franz i had nothing in common with that nation. I saw the same thing, more justifiably, in Warsaw at the coronation of Stanislas Augustus Poniatowski, who also fancied dressing up as a Spaniard. This costume made the old courtiers weep, but they had to swallow the pill, for under Russian despotism they were left with nothing but their ability to think.

Emperor Franz i was handsome, and I would have recognized him as such even had he not been a monarch. He had great consideration for his wife and did not hinder her prodigality, for she used only Kremnitzes when she played and paid out pensions. He let her put the country into debt because he was wise enough to become the creditor himself. He encouraged trade because he put a good portion of the profits it produced into his own coffers. He was also a ladies' man, and the empress, who always called him 'Master,' pretended not to notice. Perhaps she did not want the world to know that her charms were not enough for her husband's temperament, especially as the whole world admired the beauty of her numerous family. I thought all the archduchesses beautiful, except for the first; among the males I examined only the eldest, whose physiognomy I found unfortunate, despite the contrary opinion of Abbé Bighead, who also prided himself on being a physiognomist.

'What do you make of it?' he asked.

'I see presumption, and suicide.'

I had seen correctly, for Joseph II indeed killed himself; and although he did not do so intentionally, he killed himself nonetheless. Only his presumption prevented his realizing it. What he pretended to know, but did not know, rendered what he did know useless, and the intelligence he sought spoiled the one he possessed. He loved to converse with those who were dazzled by his reasoning but did not know how to reply, and he dismissed as pedants all those whose valid reasoning robbed his own of its force. Seven years ago at Laxenburg, while discussing someone who had spent a fortune purchasing titles of nobility, he told me that he despised those who bought them. I replied that it would be better to despise those who sold them. He turned his back on me, thereafter considering me no longer worthy of hearing his voice. He loved to see laughing, at least to themselves, those who listened to him when he told a story in society, for he was a good storyteller and pleasantly embroidered the circumstances of the subject; but he treated all those who did not laugh at his pleasantries as dull-witted. Yet it was these who understood better than the rest. He preferred the reasoning of his doctor Brambila, who was leading him to the grave, to that of his other doctors, who said *principiis obsta* ('stand firm against the onset of a malady'). His courage was beyond question. As for the art of ruling, he was ignorant of it, for he had no knowledge of the human heart. He could neither dissemble nor keep a secret; he displayed to all the pleasure he took in meting out punishment, and he never learned to control his facial expressions. Indeed he so neglected this artifice that when he saw someone he did not know, he grimaced in a way which made him quite ugly, when he could have easily masked his hateful mien with an eyeglass; for his grimace seemed to say: 'Who is *that* creature?'

This sovereign succumbed to a very cruel illness, cruel in that his mind was clear up to the end and before killing him forced him to confront his inescapable death. He must have had the misfortune to repent of all he had done, and the companion misfortune of not being able to undo what he had done, in part because it was not possible, in part because he would have considered it a dishonor, for the awareness of his high birth must have always remained on his mind, even as he lay dying. He had the greatest admiration for his brother, who today rules in his place, yet in spite of this he never had the strength to follow the principal advice his brother had given him. In his magnanimity he gave a rich reward to the intelligent doctor who had pronounced his death sentence, but only after having likewise rewarded some months earlier, with equal pusillanimity, the doctors and the charlatan who had led him to believe he was cured. He also had the misfortune of knowing that he would not be missed; and this is a distressing thought. His other misfortune was not to die before the archduchess, his niece. If those around him had truly loved him, they would have spared him the heartbreaking news of her death, for he had already been given up for lost and there was no danger that he would ever again be capable of punishing such discretion as an indiscretion. But it was feared that his successor would not be generous with the worthy lady, who immediately received a hundred thousand florins. Leopold would never have cheated anyone.

Charmed by my stay in Vienna and by the pleasures I enjoyed with the beautiful Fräuleins I had met at the home of the baroness, I was thinking of leaving when Herr Weiss found me at the wedding celebration of Count Durazzo and invited me to a picnic at Schönbrunn. And so we went, and I denied myself nothing there, but I returned to Vienna with such a powerful case of indigestion that in twenty-four hours I was at the edge of my grave.

I used the very last of what remained of my wits to save my life. At my bedside I had Campioni, in whose house I was staying, Roggendorf, and Sarotin. The latter, who had become my close friend, came with a doctor, even though I had explained that I did not want one. This doctor, believing that he could resort to the tyranny of his art, had sent for a surgeon, and they were going to bleed me without my consent. Half dead, I opened my eyes with I know not what inspiration and saw the man with his lancet about to open my veins. 'No! no!' I cried, and, losing strength, withdrew my arm. But my tormentor, in the doctor's words, was going to save my life in spite of me, and I saw them seize my arm. I quickly put my hand on one of the two pistols which I had on my nightstand, and fired it at the one who had sworn obeisance to the doctor. The ball uncurled a lock of his hair, and this was quite enough to make the surgeon, the doctor and all those around me depart. The only one who did not abandon me was the chambermaid, who gave me water to drink whenever I asked for it. Four days later I was in perfect health. The whole city of Vienna heard the story, and Abbé Bighead assured me that had I killed my tormentor, nothing would have happened to me, since the two noblemen who were present had witnessed that I was about to be bled by force. In addition, everyone told me that the doctors of Vienna were saying that had they indeed bled me, I would have died. On the other hand, I now had to take care not to fall ill, for henceforth no doctor would have dared visit me. This incident created a stir. When I went to the Opera, many asked to make my acquaintance; I was seen as a man who had fought off Death by firing a pistol at him. My friend Marol, a painter of miniatures, had died from indigestion because he had been bled, and his experience had taught me that to cure this malady one must only drink water and be patient. The distress one feels cannot be communicated. One does not want to vomit, for vomiting is no cure. I shall never forget a witticism that came from the mouth of a man who never made them, one M. de Maisonrouge, as he was being brought home dying of indigestion. A confused jam of carts near the Quinze-Vingt forced his coachman to stop. A begger came up to his carriage and asked for alms, saying that he was dying of hunger. Maisonrouge opened his eyes, looked at him and said:

'You're a very lucky rascal.'

Around this time I made the acquaintance of a Milanese ballerina who had a keen mind for literature and was pretty as well. At her house she received a fashionable crowd. There I met the likeable, rich and generous Count Christopher Erdödy and the effervescent Prince Kinsky, who had all the grace of a Harlequin. This woman, whom I believe to be still alive, kindled a passion in me, but in vain, for she had fallen in love with a dancer named Angiolini, newly arrived from Florence. I courted her, but she paid me no attention. A woman of the theater in love with another is unconquerable, unless you can win her with gold. I was not rich. In spite of this I did not despair, and continued to frequent her. She must have found my company amusing because she showed me the letters she wrote, and I praised their beauties; in so doing I would sit beside her and enjoy the beauty of her eyes. She also showed me her letters from her brother, who was a Jesuit and a preacher. She had a portrait of herself in miniature, very lifelike. On the eve of my departure, furious that I had been able to obtain nothing from this beauty, I resolved to steal her portrait, the last feeble resort of an unlucky wretch who had not been able to possess the original. Thus on the day I said goodbye to her, I took it without her noticing, and put it in my pocket. The next day I left for Pressburg, where Baron Weiss had invited me on an outing with two Fräuleins.

We got out of our carriage at an inn, and the first person I saw was the chevalier de Talvis, the same man who had forced me to give him a little cut with my sword at the Étoile the day I had written *labré* after *Condé* on the bill given me by the Swiss man's wife at the Tuileries. As soon as he saw me, he approached and said I owed him a chance at revenge. I told him that I never left one party for another, and that we would meet again.

'Fair enough,' he replied. 'Will you do me the honor of presenting me to these ladies?'

'Gladly, but not in the street.'

We went upstairs and he followed us. I was thinking that this man, who was certainly a brave sort, might provide us with some amusement, and I introduced him. He had been staying at this same inn for two days and was dressed in mourning and wearing a shirt with frayed cuffs. He asked us if we were going to the prince-bishop's ball, about which we knew nothing, and Weiss said yes.

'One need not be presented to enter,' said Talvis, 'and that is why I'm counting on going, since nobody knows me here.'

A moment later he left. The innkeeper came to take our orders and told us about the ball. The Fräuleins wanted to go, and so we did, after having a bite to eat. There were a great many people there, and since nobody knew us we walked about with complete freedom.

We entered a room where we saw a great table surrounded by the nobility, who were punting faro. The dealer was the prince, and between sovereigns and ducats the bank seemed to total some thirteen or fourteen thousand florins. Chevalier de Talvis was standing between two ladies, whom he flattered with compliments, while monsignor shuffled. Presenting the cards to be cut, he suddenly noticed the Frenchman and told him to put in a card as well.

'Gladly, monsignor; the bank on this card.'

'The bank it is,' the bishop said grandly, wanting all to see that he was not afraid, and at once the card appeared at his left and the chevalier nonchalantly gathered up all the gold. The astonished bishop said to the Gascon:

'If your card had lost, monsieur, how would you have paid me?'

'Monsignor, that is none of your concern.'

'Monsieur, you are more lucky than wise.'

Talvis left with the gold in his pockets.

This astonishing incident gave rise to countless discussions, all of which ended with the conclusion that this foreigner must be mad or desperate, and that the bishop was a fool.

Half an hour later we returned to the inn; we asked for news of the winner and were told that he had gone to bed. I said to Weiss that we should profit from this event by borrowing a small sum. We entered his room very early the next morning, and I complimented him and asked if he would be so kind as to lend me a hundred ducats.

'With all my heart.'

'I will repay you in Vienna. Would you like a receipt?'

'No receipt.'

He counted out a hundred Kremnitz ducats, and a quarter-hour later he left for Vienna by post. His only possessions were an overnight bag, a frock coat and a pair of boots. I divided the hundred ducats fairly among the four of us, and we returned to Vienna the next day. We found this story on the lips of all of high society, but nobody knew that we had received a hundred ducats nor that the winner was the chevalier de Talvis; nor could anyone in Vienna, until that moment, have guessed who the man might be. Nobody at the French ambassador's had any idea. I never did hear any subsequent news of him. I left with the diligence and after four days of travel reached Trieste, where I immediately embarked for Venice. I arrived there two days before the feast of the Ascension in 1753.

[...]

[*By June of 1753, Casanova is back in Venice, where he finds Teresa Imer once again and, more importantly, meets the very young 'C.C.' (Caterina Capretta), with whom he falls so much in love that he asks his friend and patron Bragadin for permission to marry. Her parents are against it, however, and the girl is shut up in a convent on the Venetian island of Murano. Giacomo, meanwhile, between gains and losses at gambling and a risky partnership in a faro bank with the adventurer and swindler Antonio della Croce, manages repeatedly to visit her. Croce is soon banished from Venice, and Casanova keeps busy trying to rescue C.C., who has meanwhile suffered a hemorrhage from an abortion. During his frequent visits to the convent, he is noticed by another nun (called only 'M.M.' in the narrative). Replying to an anonymous letter from her, he becomes involved in an affair that is one of the most famous and important episodes of his story.]*

Indulging the Senses

Nothing is more precious to the thinking man than life itself; yet in spite of this, the greatest voluptuary is he who best practices the difficult art of making it pass quickly. It is not that he wishes to make life briefer; rather, he wants amusement to make him unaware of its passing. And he is right, so long as he does not shirk his duties. Those who think they have no duties other than to indulge the senses are mistaken; it is possible that Horace, too, was mistaken when he told Julius Florus: *Nec metuam quid de me judicet heres. Quod non plura datis inveniet.* ('Nor will I fear the judgment of my heir when he does not receive more than I did.') The happiest man is he who best understands the art of finding happiness without letting it encroach upon his duties; and the unhappiest is he who has chosen a way of life in which he finds himself with the sad obligation to plan every day, from morning till night.

Certain that M.M. (The 'nun of Murano', probably Marina Maria Morosini) would not go back on her word, I went to the convent's visiting room two hours before noon. The way I looked made her ask immediately if I was ill.

'No,' I replied, 'but I have been so anxious waiting for an all-consuming happiness that I may well look ill. I have lost my appetite, and the ability to sleep; if it is postponed, I cannot answer for my life.'

'Nothing has been postponed, dear friend; but what impatience! Let us be seated. Here is the key to the *casino* to which you will go. There will be people there, for we must be served; but no one will speak to you, and you need not speak to anyone either. You shall wear a mask. You will not go there until *half-past the night's first hour*, not before. You shall climb the stairway next to the front door, and at the top of the staircase, by the light of a lantern, you will see a green door, which you shall open to enter an apartment that you will find illuminated. You will find me in the second room, and if I am not there, wait for me. I shall only be a few minutes. You may take off your mask, warm yourself by the fire and read, for you will find books there. The door to the casino is at such and such a spot.'

Her description could not have been more exact, and I rejoiced that I could not lose my way. I kissed the hand that had given me the key, and the key as well, before putting it in my pocket. I asked her if I would see her in lay dress or in her present holy attire.

'I shall leave dressed as a nun, but in the casino I shall be in lay clothes. There I will also have everything I need to disguise myself.'

'I hope you will not be in lay dress this evening.'

'And why, if I may ask?'

'I so like you coiffed as you are.'

'Ah, I see. Since you imagine I have no hair, I must frighten you. Rest assured I have the finest wig possible.'

'My God! What are you saying? The mere mention

of a wig overwhelms me. But no, have no fear; I shall find you charming in any case. Just be careful not to put it on in my presence. You seem mortified. I beg your pardon. I am sorry to have brought it up. Are you certain no one will see you leave the convent?'

'You can rest assured; when you circle round the island by gondola, you will see a little quay. It gives onto a room to which I have the key; the lay sister who serves me is trustworthy.'

'What about the gondola?'

'My lover vouches for the gondoliers.'

'Your lover is quite a man! He must be old.'

'Actually, no. I would be ashamed. I am certain he is under forty. He has everything, my dear, to make him worthy of love: beauty, wit, sweetness of character and fine manners.'

'And he pardons your caprices.'

'What are you calling caprices? He had his way with me a year ago. I knew no man before him, just as no one before you has inspired my fantasies. When I told him everything, he was a bit surprised; then he laughed and gently scolded me on the risk I would run were I to give myself to someone indiscreet. He would have liked at least for me to know who you were before going any further, but it was too late. I vouched for you, and he laughed to hear me vouch for someone I did not know.'

'When did you confide all this to him?'

'The day before yesterday, and I told him the whole truth. I showed him copies of my letters, and yours, which, when he read them, made him think you were

37

French, although you told me you are Venetian. He is curious to know who you are, no more. But since I myself am not curious, you have nothing to fear. I give you my word of honor that I shall never make the slightest attempt to find out.'

'Nor I to know who this man is, though he is as unusual as you are. When I think of the pain I have caused you, it drives me to despair.'

'Let's not speak of it; but take heart, for when I think about it, I realize that you could not have acted otherwise, unless you were a fool.'

As I took my leave she pledged her tenderness to me once again at the little window, where she remained until I left the visiting room.

That evening, at the appointed time, I found the casino without the slightest difficulty, opened the door and, following her instructions, found her dressed in the most elegant lay clothes. The chamber was illuminated by candles in holders placed before mirrored panels, and by three other candelabra on a table covered with books. M.M. seemed to me a completely different type of beauty from the one I saw in the convent's visiting room. Her hair was coiffed in a chignon accentuating its thickness, but my eyes merely glanced at it, for nothing would have been more foolish at that moment than to compliment her fine wig. Kneeling before her, bearing witness a hundred times to my gratitude by continuously kissing her beautiful hands, such would have been the preludes to the transports of a classical amorous combat, had M.M. not imagined it her first duty to defend herself. Such charming refusals!

The strength of the two hands repelling the attacks of a respectful, tender lover, at once bold and insistent, interfered only slightly. The weapon with which she preferred to check my passion and restrain my fire was reason itself, meted out in words as passionate as they were energetic, and fortified at every turn with loving kisses that melted my soul. We spent two hours in this struggle, as sweet as it was difficult for us both. At the end of this battle, we congratulated each other, each claiming victory over the other; she for having defended herself from my attacks, me for having kept my impatience in check.

At four o'clock (I am still counting in Italian time), she told me she was famished and hoped I was too. She rang, and a well-dressed woman, neither young nor old and with an honest face, set a table for two. Putting all that we might need on another table beside us, she served the meal. The dinner service was of Sèvres china. The meal was composed of eight courses, each of them brought out atop a silver box filled with hot water to keep it warm. The food was delicate and refined. I exclaimed that the cook must be French, and she confirmed this. We drank only Burgundy, and emptied a bottle of 'partridge eye' Champagne and another of sparkling wine to lighten our spirits. She dressed the salad; her appetite was equal to my own. She did not ring again except to call for dessert and everything we needed to make punch. I had to admire the knowledge, poise and grace in everything she did. It was obvious she had a lover who had taught her. I found myself so curious to know who he was that

I told her I was ready to tell her my name if she would only tell me that of the lucky man whose heart and soul she possessed. She answered that we should leave the task of satisfying our curiosity to time.

Among the charms on her watch she had a small rock crystal flask identical to the one I had on my watch chain. I showed it to her, praising the essence of rose that emanated from a small piece of saturated cotton inside it. She showed me hers, which was filled with the same essence in liquid form.

'I am surprised,' I told her, 'since it is very rare and costly.'

'And it cannot be bought.'

'Indeed the essence was created by the king of France; he made a pound of it that cost him ten thousand ecus.'

'Mine was a present someone gave to my lover, who gave it to me.'

'Mme. de Pompadour sent a little vial of it two years ago to Signor Mocenigo, the Venetian ambassador to Paris, through the A. de B., who is currently the French ambassador here.'

'Do you know him?'

'I met him that day and had the pleasure of dining with him. On the eve of his departure, on his way here, he came to say goodbye. He is a man favored by fortune, but likewise a man of merit and wit, and of distinguished birth, for he is the count of Lyons. His pretty face earned him the nickname of "Belle-Babet"; he has also published a small collection of verse that does him honor.'

Midnight had struck, and time became precious. We

left the table, and in front of the fire I grew insistent. I told her that even if she did not want to yield to love, she could not refuse nature, which must be urging her to lie down after so pleasant a supper.

'So you are sleepy?'

'Not at all, but one usually goes to bed at this hour. Let me put you to bed and sit at your bedside, or else allow me to retire.'

'If you leave me I shall be very unhappy.'

'Certainly not more than I would be in leaving you; but what shall we do beside the fire until daybreak?'

'We can both sleep in our clothes on the sofa you see before you.'

'In our clothes? So be it. I can even let you sleep; but will you forgive me if I cannot sleep? At your side, and constricted by my clothing, how could I hope to sleep?'

'Very well. In fact this sofa is a proper bed. You shall see.'

She got up, pulled the sofa out at an angle, spread out the pillows, sheets and covers, and I saw a proper bed. She tucked my hair into a large handkerchief, and gave me another so that I could do the same for her, telling me she had no nightcap. Masking my distaste for her wig, I set about this task when I was greatly surprised by something utterly unexpected. Instead of a wig I found the finest head of hair. After a hearty laugh, she told me a nun had no other duty than to hide her hair from the profane; so saying, she threw herself down, fully extended, on the sofa. I quickly removed my coat, kicked my shoes from my feet, and fell more on top of her than beside her. She held me in her arms, and exercising an unnatural tyranny over herself, she hoped I would forgive her all the torments her resistance must be causing me.

With a trembling and timid hand, and watching her with eyes that begged for mercy, I untied the six wide ribbons that closed her dress in front, delighted that she did not stop me, and found myself the happy master of the most beautiful bosom. Time was running out. She was obliged to allow me to devour it after contemplating its charms; I raised my eyes to her face and there read an amorous sweetness that said to me, *be happy with this, and learn from me to suffer abstinence.* Driven by love and all-powerful nature, and in despair because she would not allow my hands to roam elsewhere, I did everything I could to guide one of hers to the place that might persuade her that I deserved her mercy; but with a strength greater than mine, she would not move her hands from my chest, where there was nothing of interest to be found. Nonetheless, this was where her mouth landed when her lips left mine.

Out of necessity or the fatigue of spending so many hours without being able to do anything more than continuously swallow our mingled saliva, I fell asleep in her arms, holding her close in mine. I awoke with a start when I heard bells chiming.

'What was that?'

'Let us quickly dress, my loving friend; I must return to the convent.'

'You get dressed. I want to enjoy the spectacle of seeing you masked again as a saint.'

'With pleasure. If you are not in a hurry, you may sleep here.'

Then she rang for the same woman, who must have been the great confidante of all her amorous secrets. After having her hair done, she removed her dress, placed her watches, rings and all secular ornaments in a secretary that she locked; she then put on the shoes of her order, then a corset in which she enclosed in a narrow prison the pretty children who alone had nurtured me with their sweet nectar, before finally donning her habit. When the confidante had gone out to summon the gondolier, she threw her arms around my neck and told me she would wait for me the day after next; at that time she would tell me what night she could come to my house in Venice. There, she said, we would satisfy each other in full. Then she left. Very happy with my fate, although full of unfulfilled desires, I blew out the candles, and slept soundly until noon.

I left the casino without seeing a soul and, well masked, went to see Laura, who gave me a letter from C.C. (Caterina Capretta), which went something like this:

Here, my dear husband, is a good example of my way of thinking. You will find me ever more worthy of being your wife. You must, in spite of my age, consider me capable of keeping a secret, and discreet enough not to find fault in your reserve. Assured of your heart's love, I am not jealous of your mind's fancies, which help you suffer our separation patiently.

I must tell you that yesterday, as I passed through a

corridor above the convent's visiting room, I dropped a toothpick from my hand and had to pull a footstool away from the wall to look for it. As I bent down to pick it up, through an almost imperceptible crack where the floor meets the wall, I saw you yourself speaking to my dear friend Mother M.M. You cannot imagine either my surprise or my joy. These two sentiments immediately gave way to the fear of being seen and making some indiscreet soul curious. After quickly returning the footstool to its place, I left. Oh! my dear friend, I beg you to tell me everything. How could I love you and not be curious to hear the story behind this remarkable event? Tell me if she knows you, and how you met her. She is a dear friend of mine; I have spoken to you of her, but never thought it necessary to name her. It is she who taught me French, and who gave me books from her room that have educated me in an important area many women know little about. Without her, no one would have discovered the grave disease that almost killed me. She gave me linen and sheets; I owe her my honor. In all this she learned I had a lover, just as I know she has one too; but we have never been curious about our respective secrets. Mother M.M. is an incomparable woman. I am certain, dear friend, that you love her, and that she loves you too; and since I am not at all jealous, I think I deserve to know the whole story from you. But I pity you both, since anything you might manage to do can only, I think, irritate your passion. The whole convent believes you ill; I am dying to see you again. Come at least one time. Adieu.

This letter disturbed me, for although I could count on C.C., this crack could expose us to others. In addition, I now had to lie to my beloved, since love and honor prevented me from telling her the truth. In the reply I immediately sent her, I told her she must tell her friend at once that she had seen her through the crack talking to someone in a mask. As for my meeting with the nun, I told C.C. that having heard of her rare merit, I had had her called to the grating, introducing myself under an assumed name. Therefore she must refrain from mentioning me, for the nun had recognized me as the same person who went to hear Mass at her church. As for love, I assured her there was nothing between us, although I agreed that she was a charming woman.

On Ste. Catherine's day, C.C.'s name day, I went to Mass in the convent's church. As I was walking to the *traghetto* to take a gondola, I noticed I was being followed. But I needed to be certain of it. I saw the same man also take a gondola and follow me; this might have been a coincidence, but in order to make certain, I disembarked in Venice at the Palazzo Morosini del Giardino and saw the same man likewise descend. Now I was certain. I left the palace, stopped in a narrow street near the Flanders post, saw the spy, and with knife in hand forced him into a dark corner with the point at his throat, insisting he tell me on whose command he was following me. He might have told me everything had someone not appeared on the street by chance. And so he escaped and I learned nothing. But seeing that it was only too easy for a curious person to find out who I was if he so desired, I decided henceforth to go to Murano only masked, or at night.

The next day, when M.M. was supposed to tell me how she would arrange to come sup with me, I went to the convent's visiting room very early. She appeared before me beaming with the happiness flooding her soul. The first thing she said was to compliment me on appearing at her church after three weeks of absence. She told me that the Abbess had been very pleased, because she was certain she knew who I was. I then told her of the spy, and of my resolution not to attend Mass in her church any more. She replied that it would be wise for me to come to Murano as little as possible. She then told me in detail of the crack in the old floorboards, and informed me it had already been sealed. She said she had been forewarned by a boarder at the convent who was very attached to her, but did not name her.

After these small matters, I asked her if my happiness was to be postponed, and she said only by twenty-four hours, because a new lay sister had invited her to sup in her room.

'Such invitations,' she told me, 'are indeed rare, but when they do come you must honor them, or make an enemy of the person inviting you.'

'Can one not claim to be ill?'

'Yes, but then one must suffer visitors.'

'I see. If you refuse, they might suspect you've slipped out.'

'Not at all. They do not consider that a possibility.'

'Are you then the only one capable of this miracle?'

'Rest assured that I am the only one, and that gold is the all-powerful god that creates this miracle. So tell me where you would like to wait for me tomorrow two hours after sunset.'

'Can't I wait for you here in your casino?'

'No, for the person who will take me to Venice is my lover.'

'Your lover?'

'Himself.'

'How unusual. Then I shall wait for you in Piazza Santi Giovanni e Paolo behind the pedestal of the equestrian statue of Bartolomeo Colleoni of Bergamo.'

'I have never seen that statue, or that square, except in a print; but I shall be there. You've told me enough. Only very bad weather could prevent me from coming; but let's hope for clear skies. Adieu, then. We shall speak at length tomorrow evening, and if we sleep, we shall fall asleep contented.'

I had to move quickly, since I did not have a casino of my own. I hired a second rower and was in Piazza San Marco in less than a quarter of an hour. After spending five or six hours looking at a great many casini, I chose the most elegant, and therefore the most expensive. It had belonged to Lord Holderness, the English ambassador, who had sold it at a good price to a cook when he left. This man rented it to me until Easter for a hundred sequins paid in advance, on the condition that he himself would cook the dinners and suppers I might give.

The casino had five rooms, furnished in exquisite

taste. Everything in it had been made for the pleasures of love, good food, and the joys of the senses. Meals were served through a blind window set into the wall, containing a revolving dumb-waiter which filled the space completely so that masters and servants could not see one another. This room was adorned with mirrors, chandeliers and a superb pierglass above a white marble fireplace decorated with small painted tiles of Chinese porcelain, whose interest lay in their depictions of amorous couples in their natural state, kindling the imagination with their voluptuous positions. Small armchairs matched the sofas to the left and right. Another room was octagonal, and adorned entirely with mirrors, including the floor and ceiling; all these facing mirrors reflected the same objects from countless different points of view. This room adjoined an alcove with two secret doors to a dressing room on one side, and on the other a boudoir with a bathtub and an English-style water-closet. All the wainscotting was embossed in ormolu or painted with flowers and arabesques.

After telling the cook to put sheets on the bed, candles in all the chandeliers and candelabra in each room, I ordered supper for two for the same evening, assuring him that for wine I wanted only Burgundy and Champagne, and no more than eight courses, leaving the choice up to him, regardless of expense. The dessert was his choice as well. Taking the key to the front door, I warned him that when I entered I did not want to see anyone. The supper was to be ready at the second hour after sunset and served when I rang. I noticed with pleasure that the clock in the alcove had an alarm, for in spite of my love I was beginning to surrender to the sway of sleep.

After giving these orders, I went off to a milliner's shop to buy slippers and a nightcap trimmed with a double ruffle of Alençon point. I put these in my pocket. Since I was to entertain the most beautiful sultana of the Lord of the Universe, I wanted to make certain the day before that everything would be in order. Having told her I had a casino, I must not appear at all unfamiliar with it.

The cook was surprised when I arrived alone at two hours after sunset. I immediately criticized him for not having illuminated the place, since I had told him the time and he could not have had any doubt about it.

'I shall not forget a second time.'

'Light the candles, then, and serve.'

'But you told me for two.'

'Serve for two. Remain present at my supper this first time, so that I may tell you everything I find good or bad.'

The supper arrived in the dumb-waiter in good order, two dishes at a time; I commented on everything, but found everything, served on Saxon porcelain, to be excellent: game, sturgeon, truffles, oysters and perfect wines. I reproached him only for having forgotten to put hard-boiled eggs, anchovies and mixed oil and vinegar on a plate for the salad. He looked up to heaven contritely, accusing himself of a great mistake. I also told him that next time I would like to have bitter oranges to flavor the punch, and that I wanted rum, not arrack. After two hours at table, I told him to bring me the list of expenses. He brought it fifteen minutes later, and I was quite content. After paying, I ordered him to bring me coffee when I rang, and then retired to an excellent bed in the alcove. The bed and the fine supper rewarded me with the sweetest sleep possible. Otherwise the thought that I was to have my goddess beside me in this very bed the following night would not have let me fall asleep. Next morning as I left, I told my man I wanted all the fresh fruits he could find for dessert, and ices in particular. To keep the day from seeming too long, I gambled until evening and found my luck no different from my love. Everything went exactly as I wished. With all my heart I thanked the mighty genius of my beautiful nun for this.

I went to wait beside the statue of the hero Colleoni at the first hour after sunset. She told me to go there the second hour, but I wanted to have the sweet pleasure of waiting for her. The night was cold but magnificent, without the faintest wind.

At precisely two hours after sunset, I saw a gondola with two oarsmen arrive. A man in a mask emerged and after speaking to the gondolier at the prow, came toward the statue. Seeing a masked man, I became alarmed, dodged him, and was sorry not to have brought along my pistols. The masker walked around the statue, came up to me, and held out a peaceful hand, which calmed all my doubts. I recognized my angel dressed as a man. She laughed at my surprise, took my arm, and without a word we made our way to

Piazza San Marco, which we crossed, and went to the casino, which was only about thirty paces from the Teatro San Moisè.

Everything was as I had arranged. We went upstairs and I quickly removed my mask, but M.M. amused herself by slowly exploring all the nooks and crannies of the delicious place into which she had been received, charmed to let me contemplate from every angle, and often straight on, all the graces of her person, and admire in her finery the lover who possessed her. She was surprised by the marvel of seeing herself from one hundred vantage points all around her and at the same time, even though she stood still. The multiple portraits that the mirrors offered her in the light of all the carefully placed candles were a novel spectacle that made her fall in love with herself. Seated on a stool, I attentively examined the elegance of her attire. She wore a coat of rose-colored cut velvet, trimmed with embroidered gold spangles, a matching hand-embroidered waistcoat that could not have been more sumptuous, black satin breeches, needlelace ruffles, buckles studded with brilliants, a priceless solitaire on her little finger, and on the other hand a ring with a surface of white taffeta covered with a convex crystal. Her *bautta* of black blond-lace was as handsome as could be in its fineness and design. She came and stood in front of me so that I could see her better. I looked through her pockets, and found a snuffbox, comfit box, flagon, a case of toothpicks, a pair of opera glasses, and handkerchiefs that filled the air with pleasant scents. I attentively examined the richness and workmanship of her two watches and her handsome signets hung as pendants from chains covered with small diamonds. When I looked in her side pockets, I found flat flintlock pistols with spring firing mechanisms, of the finest English workmanship.

'Everything I see,' I told her, 'is unworthy of you, but allows my astonished soul to pay homage to the adorable man who wants you to know that you are truly his mistress.'

'That is what he said when I asked him to bring me to Venice and leave me here. He added that he wanted me to amuse myself, so that I would be all the more convinced that the man I was to make happy deserved it.'

'That is incredible, my dear friend. A lover of this stamp is rare indeed, for I could never deserve the happiness that already so bedazzles me.'

'Let me go unmask myself alone.'

Fifteen minutes later, she appeared before me, coiffed as a man but with her handsome hair unpowdered, the long curls grazing her chin on either side of her face. A black ribbon tied it behind her neck, letting it hang in a loose plait down to her knees. As a woman, M.M. resembled Henriette, and as a man a guardsman I once knew in Paris named *l'Etorière*; or even Antinoüs, of whom one still sees statues, had her French garb allowed me the illusion.

Overwhelmed by so many charms, I thought I was going to faint. I threw myself on the sofa to support my head.

'I have lost all faith,' I told her. 'You will never be

mine. Even tonight some fateful mishap will tear you from my arms, perhaps some miracle wrought by your divine husband in jealousy of a mortal. I feel annihilated. In one quarter of an hour I may no longer exist.'

'Are you mad? I am yours this very instant, if you like. Although I've not eaten today, I am not the least bit hungry. Let us go to bed.'

She was cold, so we sat down before the fire. She told me she had not worn a waistcoat. I unfastened a diamond heart that closed her ruffle, and my hands sensed, before my eyes saw, that only her chemise shielded the cold from the two sources of life adorning her bosom. I grew ardent; but it took only a single kiss of hers to calm me, and two words: 'After supper.'

I rang and, seeing her alarm, showed her the dumb-waiter.

'No one will see you,' I told her, 'you might tell your lover, who is perhaps unaware of this device.'

'He is not unaware of it; but he will admire your attention and note that you are not a novice in the art of pleasing, and that clearly I am not the only woman to enjoy the delights of this little house with you.'

'And he will be wrong. I have not dined or slept here with anyone else; and I abhor lies. You are not my first passion, my divine friend, but you shall be my last.'

'I shall be happy, my friend, if you are faithful. My lover is faithful and sweet; but he has always left my heart untouched.'

'His heart must be untouched as well, for were his love of the same cast as mine, he would never allow you an absence such as this. He could not tolerate it.'

'He loves me, as I love you. Do you believe I love you?'

'I must believe it; but you would not tolerate –'

'Say no more; for I sense that so long as you do not hide things from me, I shall forgive you everything. The joy I feel in my soul right now comes more from the certainty that I possess what is necessary to fulfill your every desire, than from the idea that I am about to spend a delicious night with you. It will be the first such night of my life.'

'You have not spent such nights with your worthy lover?'

'Yes. But they were animated only by friendship, gratitude and kindness. Love is what truly counts. In spite of this my lover is very much like you. He has a lively wit, equal to your own, and a comely face and figure as well, though he does not look at all like you. I think he is even richer than you, although to judge from this casino one might suspect the opposite. But do not imagine that I deemed you less deserving than he because you have confessed yourself incapable of the heroism of allowing me an absence. On the contrary, if you told me you would indulge one of my fantasies as he has, I would know that you did not love me as you do, for which I am very grateful.'

'Will he be curious about the details of this night?'

'He will think it pleases me to be asked how it went, and I shall tell him everything except a few small details that might humiliate him.'

After the supper, which she found both delicate and exquisite, as she did the ices and oysters, she made punch. After drinking a few glasses of it, in my amorous impatience I begged her to consider the fact that we had but seven hours ahead of us and would be doing ourselves a great injustice not to spend them in bed. Thus we went into the alcove, which was lighted by twelve blazing candles, and from there into the dressing room, where I presented her with the beautiful lace nightcap and requested that she comb her hair as a woman. Proclaiming the nightcap magnificent, she told me to go undress in the next room, promising to call me as soon as she was in bed.

This took but two minutes. I threw myself into her burning arms, passionate with love, and gave her the most ardent proof of this for seven hours straight, interrupted only by as many quarter hours animated by the tenderest exchanges. She taught me nothing new in matters of the act itself, but countless novelties in the way of sighs, ecstasies, transports and natural sentiments that arise only in such moments. Each discovery I made raised my soul to love, which in turn fortified me in the demonstration of my gratitude. She was astonished to find herself receptive to so much pleasure, for I showed her many things she had considered fictions. I did things to her that she did not feel she could ask me to do, and I taught her that the slightest constraint spoils the greatest pleasures. When the morning bells tolled, she raised her eyes to the Third Heaven like an idolatress thanking the Mother and Son for having so well rewarded the effort it had cost her to declare her passion to me.

We dressed in haste, and seeing me place the beautiful nightcap in her pocket, she assured me she would cherish it forever. After coffee, we walked at a brisk pace to Piazza Santi Giovanni e Paolo, where I left her, assuring her she would see me in two days' time. After watching her get in her gondola, I went home and, after ten hours of sleep, returned to my natural state.

Awaiting a Lover

Two days later I went to the convent's visiting room after dinner. I sent for her, and she came at once and told me to go away, for she was awaiting her lover, but to come without fail the next day. I left. At the end of the bridge, I saw a poorly masked man emerge from a gondola, whose oarsman I recognized as being in the service of the ambassador of France. He was not in livery, and the gondola was as simple as all those belonging to Venetians. I turned my head and saw the mask go into the convent. I no longer had any doubts, and I returned to Venice delighted to have made this discovery and enchanted that my principal was the ambassador. I decided not to mention it to M.M.

When I saw her the next day, she told me her lover had come to take leave of her until Christmas time.

'He is going to Padua,' she told me, 'but everything has been arranged for us to sup at his casino if we wish.'

'Why not go to Venice?'

'Not until he returns. He made me promise. He is a very prudent man.'

'Of course. When shall we next sup at the casino?'

'On Sunday, if you like.'

'Sunday it is; I shall go to the casino at dusk, and

read while waiting for you. Did you tell your lover it was not unpleasant at my casino?'

'My dear friend, I told him everything; but one thing disturbed him a great deal. He wants me to beg you not to expose me to the danger of pregnancy.'

'Perish the thought. But do you not run the same risk with him?'

'Not at all.'

'Then we must be careful in the future. I think that nine days before Christmas, since we will not have masks I shall be obliged to come to your casino by water, since on foot I could easily be recognized as the same person who attends your church.'

'That is very prudent of you. I can show you the quay very easily. I hope you will likewise be able to come here during Lent, when God asks us to mortify our senses. Isn't it droll that there is a time when the Lord thinks it good for us to amuse ourselves, and another in which we can only please him by abstinence? What could an anniversary have to do with divinity? I do not know how the action of the creature can influence the creator, whom my reasoning can only conceive of as independent. It seems to me that had God made man capable of offending him, man would be right to do everything forbidden to him, if only to help Him learn how to create. Can you imagine God unhappy during Lent?'

'My divine love, you reason beautifully; but might I ask where you learned to reason, and how you managed to take such a step?'

'My lover gave me many books, and the light of

truth burned through the clouds of superstition weighing down upon my intellect. I assure you that when I think about myself, my happiness at having found someone to enlighten me is greater than my unhappiness at having taken the veil, since the greatest pleasure is to live and die peacefully, which we cannot hope to do if we believe what the priests tell us.'

'How true. But let me admire you, since the task of enlightening a mind so prejudiced as yours must have been at the time could not have been accomplished in only a few months.'

'I would have seen the light a lot less soon had I been less filled with misconceptions. What separated the true from the false in my mind was merely a veil; only reason itself could lift it, but I had been taught to disdain reason. Once I was shown that I must make the most of it, I put it to work at once, and the veil was lifted. The truth suddenly became clearly manifest, and all my silly notions disappeared. I need not worry that they will reappear, for I fortify myself against them daily. I can say that I did not begin to love God until I disabused myself of the idea religion had given me of Him.'

'Congratulations. You have been more fortunate than I. You have made more progress in one year than I have in ten.'

'So you did not begin by reading what Lord Bolimbroke has written? Five or six months ago I was reading Charron's *La Sagesse* and I don't know how our confessor found out. He had the audacity to tell me during confession that I should stop reading it. I responded that since it did not disturb my conscience, I could not obey him. He told me he would not absolve me, and I answered that I would take communion anyway. The priest went to Bishop Diedo to ask what he should do, and the bishop came to talk to me, insinuating that I should follow my confessor. I told him that my confessor's job was to absolve me, and that he had no right to give me unsolicited advice. I told him outright that it was his duty not to create a scandal in the convent, and that if he would not absolve me, I would take communion anyway. The bishop told him to leave me to my own conscience. But I was not satisfied. My lover obtained a papal brief allowing me to confess myself to whomever I pleased. All my sisters are jealous of this privilege; but I have used it only once, since it is not worth the trouble. I still confess to the same priest, who after hearing me out has no problem absolving me, since I tell him nothing of any importance.'

Thus did I come to recognize a charming freethinker in this woman; yet it could not have been otherwise, since she needed more to pacify her conscience than to satisfy her senses.

After assuring her she would find me at the casino, I returned to Venice. Sunday after dinner, I circled the island of Murano in a gondola with two oarsmen, as much to see where the casino's quay might be, as to find the small quay by which she left the convent. But I could not make out a thing. I did not find the casino's quay until the novena, and the convent's small quay until six months later, at great risk to my life.

About an hour after sunset I went to the temple of

my love, and while awaiting my idol's arrival, I amused myself examining the books that made up the small library in the boudoir. They were few but well-chosen. It contained everything the wisest philosophers had written against religion, and all that the most voluptuous minds had penned on the unparalleled subject of love. These were seductive books whose incendiary style drives the reader to seek reality, the only possible means of quelling the fires he feels circulating in his veins. Besides these books, there was an *in folio* containing only erotic prints. Their great merit lay more in the beauty of their execution than the lewdness of the positions depicted. I recognized engravings for the *Portier des Chartreux* made in England, as well as others for Meursius or Aloysia Sigea Toletana, which were more beautiful than anything I had ever seen. Aside from these, the room was decorated with small paintings so well-executed that the figures seemed alive. An hour went by in no time.

When M.M. appeared dressed as a nun, I cried out. I told her, as I flung my arms around her neck, that she could not have come more fittingly attired to prevent the adolescent masturbation to which everything I had seen the previous hour would have driven me.

'But in your saintly dress you astonish me. Allow me to adore you on the spot, my angel.'

'I shall don my lay attire at once. I need but fifteen minutes. I do not like myself in these woolens.'

'Not at all. You shall receive my amorous homage in the clothing you wore when you first kindled it.'

'She answered me with the most devout *fiat voluntas*

61

tua ('Thy will be done') as she dropped onto the large sofa, where I had maneuvered her despite her resistance. Afterwards, I helped her to undress and to put on a simple shift of Peking muslin, which was as elegant as could be. Next I became her lady-in-waiting as she arranged her hair in a nightcap.

After supper, before we went to bed, we resolved not to see each other until the first day of the novena when masks are not worn, since the theaters are closed for ten days. She then gave me the keys to the door giving onto the quay. A blue ribbon tied to the window above it would be the signal that would allow me to recognize it by day, so that I could go there later by night. But what delighted her no end was that I had gone to live in the casino and would not leave until her lover's return. In the ten days I stayed there I had her four times, and thus convinced her I lived for her alone. I amused myself by reading and by writing to C.C., although my tenderness for her had abated. The main thing that interested me in the letters she wrote me was what she said about her dear friend, the mother M.M. She told me I was wrong not to have cultivated her friendship, and I answered that I had not done so out of fear of being recognized. In this way I made her all the more obliged to keep my secret to herself alone.

It is not possible to love two women at the same time, nor is it possible to maintain a strong love by feeding it too much or not at all. What kept my passion for M.M. always at the same intensity was the fact that I could never have her without the greatest fear of losing her. I told her that inevitably, sooner or later, some nun would need to speak to her at a moment when she was neither in her room nor in the convent. She assured me that this could not happen, since nothing was more respected in the convent than a nun's freedom to shut herself in her room and make herself inaccessible even to the abbess. She had nothing to fear but the fateful event of a fire, when everything becomes so confused that it would be unnatural for a nun to remain calm and detached, and so they would inevitably notice her absence. She was pleased to have won over the lay sister, the gardener, and another nun whom she never wanted to name to me. Her lover's skill and money had guaranteed this arrangement, and he answered for the faithfulness of the cook and his wife, who were the casino's guardians. He also vouched for his gondoliers, although one of them must certainly be a spy of the State Inquisitors.

On Christmas Eve she told me her lover was about to arrive, and that on St. Stephen's day she was to go to the opera with him and sup with him at the casino on the third day of Christmas. After telling me she would expect me for supper on the last day of the year, she gave me a letter, requesting that I wait until I got home to read it.

An hour before daybreak, I packed my belongings and went to the Bragadin palace. I was impatient to read the letter she had given me and immediately shut myself in my room. It said:

I was somewhat hurt, my love, when the day before yesterday, in regard to the secret I must keep from you concerning my lover, you said that although you are content to possess my heart, you leave me mistress of my mind. This division of heart and mind is a fallacious distinction, and even if you do not see it this way, you must agree that you do not love me completely, since it is impossible for me to exist without my mind, and for you to cherish my heart if my mind is not in accord with it. If your love can content itself with the contrary, it is not of the most delicate.

But since you could, one day, convince me that I haven't been as sincere with you as true love demands, I have decided to reveal a secret regarding my lover to you, although I know that he is convinced I shall never reveal it, since it would be a betrayal. You shall not, however, love me any the less for it. I find myself forced to choose between the two of you, and to betray one or the other; love has won out, but not blindly. You shall weigh the reasons that have tipped the scale in your favor.

When I could no longer resist the desire to know you more intimately, I could not satisfy myself without confiding in my lover. I never doubted he would comply with my wishes. He formed a very favorable opinion of your character when he read your first letter, in which you chose the convent's visiting room for our meeting, and he found you honorable when, after we became acquainted, you chose the casino in Murano over your own. But as soon as he learned this, he also asked me to allow him to be present at our first meeting, in a perfect hiding-place from which he would not only see what we did without being seen, but also hear everything we

said. It is an utterly secret room. You did not find it
during the ten days you spent in the casino; but I will
show it to you on the last day of the year. You tell me if
I could have refused him this pleasure. I agreed to it, and
it seemed only natural to leave you in the dark. Now
you know that my lover was present for everything we
said and did during our first encounter. But please do
not let this disturb you, my dearest. He liked you; not
only for the way you acted, but for all the charming
things you said to make me laugh. I became anxious
when the conversation turned to the type of character my
lover must have to tolerate such excessiveness; but luckily
everything you said was flattering to him. This is the
complete confession of my betrayal, which as a good lover
you must forgive me all the more as it did you no harm.
I can assure you that my lover is very curious indeed to
know who you are. That night you were natural and
very likable; had you known you were to have a witness,
God knows how you might have acted. Had I told you
about it, it is quite possible you would not have
consented, and you might have been right.

But now I must risk everything to put my mind at
ease, so that I may be exempt from reproach hereafter.
You should know, my dearest, that on the last day of the
year my lover will be at the casino, and that he will not
leave until the following day. You will not see him, but
he will see everything. Since you are not supposed to
know this, you can imagine how natural you must
appear, for if you do not, my lover will suspect I have
betrayed him, since he is very intelligent. The thing you
must keep foremost in mind is to be careful of what you

*say. He is virtuous in every area except the theological
subject of faith, and in this you have free rein. You may
speak of literature, travels, politics and tell as many
anecdotes as you like, and be assured of his approval.*

*It is up to you to decide if you are willing to allow a
man to see you during the moments you surrender
yourself to love's passions. This uncertainty now
torments me. Yes or no? There is no middle ground. Do
you understand how cruelly I am beset by doubt? Do you
understand how difficult it was for me to decide what I
should do? I shall not sleep tonight. I shall have no rest
until I read your answer. If you reply that it is not
possible for you to express passion in the presence of
someone else, especially if he is a stranger, I shall then
decide what course to take. Yet I hope that you will come
all the same, and if you cannot play the role of lover like
the first time, no unwanted consequences will ensue. For
he will believe, and I shall let him believe, that your
love has cooled.*

This letter greatly surprised me; then after thinking it
over, I laughed out loud. But it would not have made
me laugh had I not known the sort of man who was
to witness my amorous exploits. Certain that M.M.
would be very uneasy until she received my response,
I answered her at once, in the following terms:

*My divine angel, I want you to receive my answer
before noon. You shall dine without the slightest worry.*

*I shall pass the last night of the year with you. And
I promise you that your lover, whose spectacle we shall*

*be, will see and hear nothing to make him think for a
moment that you told me his secret. Rest assured that
I shall play my role to perfection. If it is a man's duty
to be ever the slave to his reason, and if, so long as he
depends on it, he should never undertake anything
without it as his guide, I shall never understand how a
man could be ashamed for a friend to see him give the
greatest proof of his love to a beautiful woman. This is
my position. You should know, however, that I think it
would have been a mistake to tell me the first time. I
would have categorically refused. I would have thought
it a slight to my honor; I would have thought that in
inviting me to supper you were merely obliging your
lover, an unusual man, for whom this predilection was
perhaps pronounced, and I would have formed so
unfavorable an impression of you that it might have
cured me of my love, which at that moment was just
beginning to bud. Such, my charming friend, is the
human heart; but now the situation is different. All that
you have told me of your worthy lover has allowed me to
understand his character, and I think of him as my
friend as well, and I love him. If no sense of shame
prevents you from letting him see you show your love
and tenderness to me, how could I, far from feeling
ashamed, not feel proud? What man would blush at his
own glory? I cannot blush, my dearest, for having won
your heart, nor for allowing myself to be seen during
moments in which I flatter myself that I shall not appear
unworthy of this favor. I do, however, know from
natural sentiment, to which reason cannot object, that
most men find it distasteful to be seen during such*

moments. Those who cannot give good reasons for this repugnance must share some of the characteristics of a cat; they may indeed have good reasons, but simply do not feel obliged to account for them to anyone.

The first of such reasons might be that a third person looking on, and visible to them, would distract them, and any distraction might lessen the pleasure of coupling.

Another important reason, which could be considered legitimate, would be that the actors might think the means by which their pleasures were gained could arouse pity in the spectators who witnessed them. Such unhappy souls are right not to seek to rouse feelings of pity in an act that seems instead designed to make others jealous. But we know, my dear, that we shall certainly not rouse feelings of pity. Everything you have told me makes me certain that your friend's angelic spirit will, in seeing us, share our pleasures. But do you know what will happen? And I shall be sorry for this, since your lover can only be a man most worthy of love. As he watches us he will become enflamed, or he will run away, or he will find himself obliged to come out of his niche, go down on bended knee before me, and beg me to surrender you to the violence of his desires, desperate to quell the fire that our revels will have kindled in his soul. If such a thing happens I shall laugh, and relinquish you to him; but I shall leave, since I sense that I could not remain a calm spectator to what another man might do to you. So adieu, my angel; everything will be fine. I will seal this letter at once, and take it to your casino in all haste.

I spent these six holidays with friends, at the Ridotto, which during that period opened its doors on St. Stephen's day. As I could not deal, since only patricians in official dress were allowed to hold the bank, I played from morning till night, and lost continuously. He who punts can only lose. But the loss of my entire fortune of four or five thousand sequins only intensified my love.

In 1774 the Great Council passed a law prohibiting all games of chance, and closed what was called the Ridotto. The Great Council was then astonished to learn, upon tallying its votes, that it had passed a law it should not have, since at least three quarters of the voters did not want it passed. Yet in spite of this at least three quarters of the ballots showed that they did. The voters looked at one another in astonishment. It was clearly a miracle of the glorious Evangelist St. Mark, who was invoked by Signor Flangini, First Corrector at the time and now Cardinal, and by the three State Inquisitors.

On the appointed day, at the usual hour, I arrived at the casino, where I found the beautiful M.M., dressed as a woman of society, standing with her back to the fireplace.

'My friend has not yet arrived,' she said, 'but I shall wink to you when he is inside.'

'Where is the place?'

'There. Notice the back of that sofa against the wall. All the raised flowers you see on it have pierced centers through which one can see from the room behind it. There is a bed there, a table, and everything a man might need to stay there for seven or eight hours, amusing himself by watching what goes on in here. You shall see it when you like.'

'Did he have it made himself?'

'Actually, no; he had no idea he would ever want to use it.'

'I realize this spectacle may give him great pleasure; but when he finds he cannot have you at the moment nature makes him most desperately need you, what will he do?'

'That is his concern. In any case he is free to leave if he becomes bored, and he can sleep too. But if you are natural he will be amused.'

'I will be natural, but more polite.'

'No politeness, my dear, for that would hardly be natural. When have you seen two lovers trouble to be polite when given over to the passions of love?'

'You are right, my love; but I will be delicate.'

'Please do. You are always delicate. Your letter pleased me; your insights went to the heart of the matter.'

M.M. was wearing nothing in her hair, which was loosely arranged. A quilted sky-blue dress was her only attire. She wore small earrings studded with brilliants, and her neck was bare. A light silk gauze and silver thread shawl, donned hastily, exposed the full beauty of her bosom and highlighted the whiteness of her skin against the front of her dress. She was wearing slippers. Her shyly smiling, modest face seemed to say, 'Here is the woman you love.' What I found extraordinary, and what pleased me greatly, was the excess of rouge, applied in the manner of the court ladies at Versailles. The charm of these painted cheeks lies in the negligence with which the color is applied. It is not intended to appear natural, but rather to please the eyes, which see in it the signs of an intoxication that promises abandon and the transports of love. She told me she had put on rouge to please her lover, who liked it. I told her that judging from this taste, I was tempted to suspect he was French. As I said these words she winked at me: her lover had arrived. The play was about to begin.

'The more I look into your eyes, the more angry I am at your husband.'

'People say he is ugly.'

'They do. He also deserves to be cuckolded; and we shall work on this all night. I have been living a celibate life for a week, but I need to eat, for my stomach is empty except for a cup of chocolate and the whites of six fresh eggs I ate in a salad dressed with oil from Lucca and Four Thieves vinegar.'

'You must be ill.'

'Yes; but I shall be fine once I have distilled them one by one in your amorous soul.'

'I did not think you were in need of stimulants.'

'Who would need them with you? But I am understandably afraid, since if I *miss* you, I shall blow my brains out.'

'What do you mean by "miss"?'

'To miss, in the figurative sense, means to fall short of one's mark. Literally it means that when I try to shoot my enemy, the pistol does not go off. I miss.'

'Ah, I see. Indeed. Well, my dark-eyed love, that would indeed be a pity, but certainly not something over which you should blow your brains out.'

'What are you doing?'

'I am removing your cloak. Give me your muff too.'

'That will be difficult, for it has been nailed.'

'What do you mean nailed?'

'Put a hand inside. See for yourself.'

'How naughty! Did the egg whites give you this nail?'

'No my angel, only your charms.'

Then I picked her up; she put her arms around my shoulders to lighten her weight. Having let the muff drop, I seized her thighs and she braced herself on the nail; but after walking all around the room, and fearing the worst, I put her down on the carpet. Then I sat down with her in my lap, and with her beautiful hand she obliged me by finishing the task, culling the first egg-white in her palm.

'Only five to go,' she said, and after cleaning her pretty hand with a potpourri of aromatic herbs, she let me shower it with a hundred kisses. Now calm, I spent the next hour amusing her with funny stories; then we sat down to eat.

She ate for two, but I for four. The service was porcelain, but for dessert it was silver gilt, as were the two candelabra of four candles each. Seeing me admire their beauty, she told me they were a gift to her from her lover.

'Did he give you candle-snuffs as well?'

'No he did not.'

'Then I judge your lover to be a great lord, since great lords do not snuff.'

'The wicks of our candles do not need to be snuffed.'

'Tell me who taught you French, for you speak too well not to make me curious.'

'Old La Forêt, who died last year. I was his student for six years; he also taught me to write verses, although I have learned words from you that I have never heard him mention, *à gogo, frustratoire, dorloter*. Where did you learn these words?'

'In Parisian high society, from such people as Mme. de Boufflers, a woman of great insight who one day asked me why *con rond* was in the Italian alphabet. I laughed heartily, but did not know what to answer her.'

'I believe those are abbreviations used in former times.'

After making punch, we amused ourselves eating oysters, exchanging them once they were already in our mouths. She presented me with hers on her tongue just as I was thrusting mine into her mouth. There is no game more lascivious, or more sensuous, that two lovers can play; it is also comical, and its comicality spoils nothing, for laughter is only intended for the happy. And how delicious the sauce dressing the oyster I sucked from my beloved's mouth! It was her saliva. The power of love could not but grow as I chewed and swallowed.

She told me she was going to change her dress and come back coiffed in her nightcap. Not knowing what else to do, I amused myself by examining the contents of her secretary, which was open. I did not touch the

Giacomo Casanova

letters, but opened a box and saw some condoms inside, which I put into my pocket. Then I hastily wrote the following lines, which I left in place of the stolen goods:

> Children of friendship, ministers of grief,
> I am Love; tremble and respect the thief.
> And you, God's wife, shrink not from motherhood;
> If you conceive, He will claim fatherhood.
> But if to me your fruits you will deny,
> Speak up; I'll unman myself to comply.

M.M. appeared in new attire, a dressing gown of Indian muslin embroidered with flowers of gold thread, and a nightcap worthy of a queen.

I threw myself at her feet, begging her to yield to my desires at once; but she ordered me to hold my fire until we were in bed.

'I do not want,' she told me laughing, 'to have to worry that your quintessence will fall on the rug. You shall see.'

Then she went to her secretary, and instead of the sheaths she found my six lines. After reading them, then reciting them out loud, she called me a thief, showering me with kisses in the hope of persuading me to return the loot. After reading my verses out loud again slowly, she pretended to think, then left under the pretext of looking for a better pen. When she returned, she wrote the following response:

> When an angel f. . .s me I've no doubts
> That nature's author is my only spouse.

But to keep His line above suspicion
Love must return my sheaths without objection.
Only as I'm subject to His holy will
May my friend f. . . me fearless, as he will.

I gave it back to her, feigning very natural shock; for it really was too much.

As midnight had struck and her little Gabriel lay pining for her, she arranged the sofa, telling me that since the alcove was too cold we would sleep there. The real reason was that in the alcove her lover would not have been able to see us.

While waiting I covered my hair in a Mazulipatan handkerchief, which, wrapped around my head four times, gave me the redoubtable look of an Asiatic despot in his harem. Having imperiously stripped my sultana to her natural state, and done the same to myself, I laid her down and subjugated her in accordance with the strictest rules, delighting in her swoons. With her buttocks raised by a pillow I had placed beneath her, and her knees bent away from the back of the sofa, she must have presented a most voluptuous sight to our hidden friend. After the revels, which lasted an hour, she removed the sheath and rejoiced to see my quintessence therein. Finding herself wet with her own distillations, we agreed that a brief ablution would restore us in *statu quo*. After this, we stood side by side in front of a tall mirror, each putting an arm behind the other's back. Admiring the beauty of our reflections, and becoming curious to play with them, we struggled in every direction, still standing. After our final bout she fell onto the Persian carpet that covered the floor. With eyes closed, head bent back, and stretched out on her back, with arms and legs spread as if she had just been cut down from a St. Andrew's cross, she would have seemed dead had the beating of her heart not been visible. The final bout had sapped her strength. I placed her in the upright tree, and in this position I lifted her up to devour her temple of love, which I could not reach otherwise, since I wished to place within her mouth's reach the weapon that had mortally wounded her without, however, taking her life.

Forced to seek a truce after this exploit, I placed her upright again; but one moment later she challenged me to a return match. It was my turn to be the upright tree, and her turn to grab my hips and raise me up. Supporting herself on her two parted columns in this position, she was horrified to see her breasts splashed with my soul distilled in drops of blood.

'What is this?' she cried, letting me fall, and falling herself with me. Then the clock chimed.

I called her back to life by making her laugh.

'Have no fear, my angel,' I told her, 'the yolk of the last egg is often red.'

I washed her beautiful breasts myself, which no human blood had soiled before that moment. She was very afraid of having swallowed a few drops of it, but I easily persuaded her that even had this been the case, no harm would come of it. She dressed in her habit and left, after telling me to sleep there and to write her before returning to Venice, to tell her how I felt. She promised to do the same the next day. The caretaker would have her letter. I did as she said. She left only after half an hour, which she certainly spent with her lover.

I slept until evening, and upon awaking I wrote her that I felt fine. I went to Venice, where I kept my promise and went to the same painter who had painted my portrait for C.C. He needed only three sittings. I asked him to make it a little larger than the first, since M.M. wanted it mounted in a medallion and covered with a holy image to hide it from the world. She alone would possess the secret of uncovering it. It would be the framer's task to make its workings different from those of the first. The same painter painted an Annunciation for me in which a dark-haired Angel Gabriel appears to a blonde Blessed Virgin, who opens her arms to the divine messenger. The famous painter Mengs used the same idea in the Annunciation he painted in Madrid twelve years later.

[...]

[*The story of Casanova's amorous relations with M.M. (possibly Marina Morosini, or Maria Eleonora Michiel) continues for several more chapters, rich in lists of the gifts exchanged (which include a portrait of Giacomo he gives the nun); in accounts of the subterfuges employed to spend evenings together at the theater and the gaming table, at times with big winnings; in descriptions of masks, disguises and balls, sometimes even inside the convent. There are also philosophical conversations between the two lovers,*

*and the usual background of complications, this time caused
by the jealousy of C.C., who learns of the love affair, takes
M.M.'s place at the pleasure-house, and finally betrays
Casanova in turn. A rich exchange of letters between
Casanova and the two women leads to a general reconcili-
ation. At the same time the protagonist becomes friends
with M.M.'s lover, whose identity he has finally confirmed:
he is Abbé Pierre de Bernis, French ambassador to Venice.
A menage à trois (and à quatre, with C.C. joining in) then
begins, between Bernis's Murano casino and Giacomo's
Venetian one; it all ends when Bernis is recalled to France.
Casanova's passions cool, only to be restoked by new amorous adventures that will involve the English ambassador
John Murray, to whom he surrenders his new young mistress Tonina, immediately replaced in his affections by her
sister Barberina. Meanwhile he suffers a series of ruinous
gambling losses. To get back on his feet, he sells, with her
consent, all of M.M.'s diamonds. But this does not resolve
his problems, and he gets further involved in shady deal-
ings, which attract the renewed suspicions of the State
Inquisitors and lead to a search of his home and immediate
incarceration in the Leads, the infamous prison under the
lead roofs of the Doge's Palace, on the night of July 25, 1755.]*

Of Appetites and Bedroom Follies

I was madly in love with my niece, who had become my mistress. My heart bled when I thought that Marseilles would become our love's tomb. All I could do was take my time getting there. From Antibes I went only as far as Fréjus in less than three hours. I told Passano to have supper with my brother and go to bed, then ordered an elegant meal and fine wines for myself and my two girls. I remained at table with them until midnight, then spent the next twelve hours in amorous frolics and sleep; I did the same in Le Luc, Brignoles and Aubagne, where I spent my sixth and last delicious night with her.

As soon as we arrived in Marseilles I took her to Mme. Audibert's after sending Passano and my brother to the *Treize Cantons*, where they were to lodge without saying a word to Mme. d'Urfé, who had been staying at the same inn for three weeks, waiting for me.

It was at Mme. Audibert's that my niece had made the acquaintance of La Croix. Madame was a spirited, scheming woman who had felt great affection for her since childhood; and it was through her mediation that my niece hoped to win her father's pardon and thus return to the bosom of her family. We had decided that she would wait in the carriage with Marcolina while I went into Mme. Audibert's house. I already knew Madame and would ask her if she knew where my niece might stay while taking the steps necessary to bring her plan to a successful conclusion.

As I climbed the stairs, Mme. Audibert, who had seen me leave the carriage from her window and was curious to know who had come to visit her by post, came to greet me. After remembering who I was, she agreed to speak with me alone inside, to find out what I might want from her. I briefly told her the essentials of the matter: the misfortune that had forced Croce to abandon Mademoiselle P.P.; (Casanova's niece) my good fortune in saving her from ruin and introducing her to someone in Genoa who would come in person to ask her father for her hand in marriage in less than two weeks; and the pleasure I felt at that very moment to be able to place this delightful creature, whom I had saved, in her charge.

'Where is she now?'

'In my carriage, where the blinds make her invisible to passers-by.'

'Have her come out, and leave everything to me. No one will know she is here. I am eager to embrace her.'

I went downstairs, drew Mlle. P.P.'s hood over her face, and led her to the waiting arms of her prudent friend, savoring this dramatic turn of events. Hugs, kisses, and tears of joy mixed with those of repentance made me weep in turn. Clairmont, as I had instructed, brought her trunk and other possessions from the carriage upstairs, and I left, promising to come see her every day.

I climbed back into my carriage after telling the

postilions where to take me: to the house of the fine old man where I had so happily kept Rosalie. Marcolina was weeping in despair to find herself separated from her dear friend. I got out at the old man's house and hastily contracted with him for Marcolina to be lodged, fed and served like a little princess. He told me he would put his own niece with her, and assured me that she would never go outside and no one would enter her rooms, which he showed me, and which I found charming.

I had her get out of the carriage and told Clairmont to follow us with her trunk.

'This,' I said, 'is your home. I shall come tomorrow evening to see if you are happy and to have supper with you. Here is your money, changed into gold. You will not be needing it, but take good care of it, for a thousand ducats in Venice will make you respectable. Do not cry, my dear Marcolina, for you have won my heart. Goodbye until tomorrow evening.'

The old man then gave me the key to the front door of his house, and I walked at a brisk trot to the *Treize Cantons*. They were expecting me, and I was led to the apartment Mme. d'Urfé had arranged for me, adjoining hers. I immediately saw Brougnole, who gave me her mistress's regards and told me she was alone and eager to see me.

It would bore the reader to read a detailed description of this meeting, for he would only find the reasonings of this poor woman, infatuated as she was with the falsest and most chimerical of doctrines, incongruous and incoherent; and my own he would find false, without a trace of truthfulness or plausibility. Given over to libertinage, and in love with the life I was leading, I took advantage of this woman's madness; had she not been my dupe, she would surely have been another's. I gave myself free rein, and played my part well. The first thing she asked me was the whereabouts of Querilinth, and she was surprised when I told her he was at the inn.

'It is he who will regenerate me in myself. I am certain of it. My genius assures me of it every night. Ask Paralis if the gifts I have prepared for him are worthy to be given by Seramis to a leader of the Rosicrucians.'

Not knowing what these gifts were, and unable to ask to see them, I answered that we must first consecrate them at the planetary hours appropriate to the ceremonies we were to perform, and that Querilinth himself could not see them before their consecration. This being so, she led me into the adjoining room, opened her secretary and withdrew seven packets which the Rosicrucian was to receive as offerings to the seven planets. Each packet contained seven pounds of metal, depending on the planet, and seven precious stones appropriate to that planet, of seven carats each: diamond, ruby, emerald, sapphire, chrysolite, topaz and opal.

Determined to proceed in such a way that none of this should fall into the hands of the Genoese Passano, I told her that, as to the method, we must rely entirely on Paralis and begin the consecration by placing each packet in a box made especially for it. We could only consecrate one a day, and had to begin with the Sun. It was a Friday, and we needed to wait until the day after next; the following day, Saturday, I had a box made with seven compartments in it. For the consecration, I spent three hours a day alone with Mme. d'Urfé, and it was not completed until a week after Saturday. During this week I had Passano and my brother join me at dinner with her; my brother understood nothing of our conversations and never said a word. Mme. d'Urfé took him for a half-wit and thought we wanted to place a sylph's soul in his body, to have him engender a creature of a species between the human and the divine. When she confided this discovery to me, she told me she would go along with it, on the condition that after the operation he would appear to have more common sense.

I took great pleasure in seeing my brother despair at being taken for a half-wit by Mme. d'Urfé, and he appeared doubly so whenever he tried say something witty to convince her of the contrary. I laughed at the thought that he would have played this role very badly had I asked him to play it on purpose; but the rascal did not fare too badly, since to amuse herself the marquise had decked him out in all the modest luxury befitting an abbé of the most illustrious family of France. The one whom the dinners with Mme. d'Urfé most distressed was Passano, who had to answer the sublime questions she put to him. Not knowing what to say, more often than not he answered evasively. He would yawn, did not dare to get drunk, and failed to observe the decency and politeness dictated by common table manners. Mme. d'Urfé told me that some great misfortune must be threatening the Order for this great man to be so distracted.

As soon as I had the box brought to Madame and we had made all the arrangements to begin the consecrations on Sunday, I had the oracle command that I was to go sleep in the country for seven consecutive days, observing total abstinence from all mortal women, and dedicate a ceremony to the Moon every night at the appropriate hour, in the open air, to prepare to regenerate Madame myself in case Querilinth was unable, for secret reasons, to perform the operation. By giving this order, not only could Mme. d'Urfé not disapprove of my sleeping elsewhere; she was actually grateful to me for the trouble I was taking to assure the success of the operation.

On Saturday, the day after my arrival in Marseilles, I went to Mme. Audibert's, where I had the pleasure of seeing Mlle. P.P. very satisfied with the kind manner in which Madame had taken her interests to heart. She had spoken to her father, telling him her daughter was with her and that the girl's sole desire was to be granted his pardon and returned to the bosom of her family, to become the wife of a rich young gentleman from Genoa, who, for the honor of his household, could receive her from his hands alone. Her father responded that he would come in two day's time to take her to stay with one of his sisters who lived in a house she owned in St.-Louis, less than two leagues from town. There she could wait calmly for her future husband to arrive, without arousing the slightest suspicion. Mlle. P.P. was surprised that her father had not yet heard from him. I told her I would not visit her in St.-Louis but would certainly see her when N.N. (A Genoese merchant whom Mlle. P.P. did, in fact, marry) arrived, and would not leave Marseilles until I had seen her married.

From there I went to see Marcolina, whom I longed to hold in my arms. She received me with heartfelt joy, telling me she would be happy except for the fact that she was unable to make herself understood, nor to understand anything the good woman who served her said. I could see that this was true, but could think of no solution. I would have needed to find her a servant who spoke Italian, and this would have been quite a chore. She was moved to tears when I gave her my niece's regards and told her that she would be in her father's arms the very next day. She already knew that she was not really my niece.

The fine, elegant supper we ate reminded me of Rosalie, whose story delighted Marcolina. She told me that it seemed I traveled solely to bring happiness to girls in distress, provided I found them pretty. Marcolina also charmed me by the appetite with which she ate. The cuisine of Marseilles is exquisite, with the exception of the poultry, which is worthless; we made do without it and forgave the garlic they put in all the dishes to give them flavor. Marcolina was charming in bed. It had been eight years since I had enjoyed Venetian follies in bed, and this girl was a masterpiece. I laughed at my brother, who was fool enough to fall in love with her. Since I could not take her anywhere but wanted her to amuse herself, I told the host to let her go to the theater with his niece every day, and to prepare supper for me every evening. The next day I dressed her up handsomely, buying her everything she might desire to shine like the other women.

The next day she told me that she had liked the play immensely, even though she could not understand a word of it. The day after that she surprised me by telling me that my brother had sat next to her in her box and said so many impertinent things to her that had she been in Venice she would have slapped him. She thought he had followed her, and feared he might become a nuisance.

Back in the inn I went to his room, where near Passano's bed I saw a man gathering up his doctor's instruments before leaving.

'What is all this? Are you ill?'

'I have caught something that will make me wiser in the future.'

'At age sixty it's a bit late.'

'There is always time.'

'You stink of medicine.'

'I'm not going anywhere.'

'That will make a bad impression on the marquise, who thinks you are a great adept.'

'*I don't give a f. . . about the marquise. Leave me alone.*'

The rascal had never spoken to me this way. I pretended not to notice and went up to my brother, who was shaving.

'What were you trying to do with Marcolina at the theater yesterday?'

'I went to remind her of her obligations and to tell her I'm not her pimp . . .'

'You insulted her, and me too. You are a miserable fool who owes everything to this charming girl, for without her I would not have bothered to look at you, and you dare say idiotic things to her?'

'I ruined myself for her; I can no longer return to Venice; I cannot live without her; and you are taking her away from me. What gives you the right to steal her?'

'The right of love, you fool, and the right of the strongest. Which is why she says she is happy with me and cannot imagine leaving me.'

'You have dazzled her, and afterward you will do to her exactly what you've done to all the others. I have the right to speak to her wherever I see her.'

'You won't speak to her again. I promise you.'

With these words I took a hackney coach to see a lawyer to find out if it was possible to have a foreign abbé who owed me money put into prison, even though I did not have the papers necessary to prove his debt.

'If he is a foreigner, you can leave a deposit, have him sequestered at the inn where he is staying, and make him pay you, unless he can prove he owes you nothing. Does he owe you very much?'

'Twelve louis.'

'Come with me to the magistrate where you shall leave twelve louis, and you will instantly be entitled to have him put under guard. Where is he staying?'

'At the same inn as I, but I don't want him to be arrested there. I shall send him to the *Ste.-Beaume*, which is a disreputable inn, and have him put under guard there. In the meantime, here are the twelve louis for the security; please draw up the warrant, and I shall see you at noon.'

'Give me his name and yours as well.'

Having done so, I returned to the *Treize Cantons*, where I found my brother fully dressed and ready to go out.

'Let's go see Marcolina,' I told him. 'You shall explain yourselves in my presence.'

'With pleasure.'

He climbed into a hackney with me, which I ordered to take us to the *Ste.-Beaume*. When we arrived, I told my brother to wait for me, assuring him I would return with Marcolina. Instead I went to the lawyer who, having already obtained the injunction, had it carried out at once. I then returned to the *Treize Cantons*, had all his things put into a trunk, and brought them to him at the *Ste.-Beaume*, where I found him in a guarded room, talking to the innkeeper, who was shocked and understood nothing. But when he saw a trunk, I took him aside and told him the entire fabricated story; he went away not wanting to hear any more. Next I entered my brother's room and told him he had better decide to leave Marseilles the next day; I said I would pay for him to go as far as Paris, but that if he would not go voluntarily, I would abandon him, after making certain, by means known to me alone, that I could have him expelled from Marseilles.

The coward began to cry and said he would go to Paris.

'You shall leave for Lyons tomorrow then; but you must first make out a paper confessing to owe the bearer twelve louis.'

'Why?'

'Because I say so. In return I promise to give you twelve louis tomorrow and tear up the note.'

'So I must blindly do everything you say?'

'It is the best you can do.'

He wrote me the note. First I went to secure him a place in the coach, and the next day I went to the lawyer to withdraw my twelve louis, which I brought to my brother, who left immediately with a letter of recommendation to M. Bono. I warned the latter not to give him any money, and to make him leave for Paris by coach. Then I gave him the twelve louis, which was more than he deserved, and tore up the note. This is how I got rid of my brother.

But the previous day, before dining alone with Mme. d'Urfé and after taking my brother's trunk to the *Ste.-Beaume*, I had gone to speak to Passano, to find out why he was in such bad spirits.

'I'm in such bad spirits because I know you are about to make off with the twenty or thirty thousand écus in gold and diamonds that the marquise had set aside for me.'

'Perhaps. But it is not for you to know if I make off with them or not. What I can tell you is that I will not allow her to commit the folly of giving you either gold or diamonds. If you think you have any claim to them, go complain to the marquise herself, I shall not try to stop you.'

'So I must suffer to have served as a go-between for your impostures without getting anything in return? Don't count on it. I want a thousand louis.'

'My compliments.'

I went to see the marquise, told her that dinner was served, and that we would dine alone, since I had been obliged to send the abbé away.

'He was an idiot. But what about Querilinth?'

'After supper Paralis will tell us everything. I have strong suspicions.'

'So do I. He seems to have changed. Where is he?'

'He is in bed with that foul disease I dare not name to you.'

'This is extraordinary. It is a work of the evil spirits, of a sort that, *I believe*, has never happened before.'

'Not so far as I know; but let us eat now. We have a lot of work to do today, after the consecration of the tin.'

'So much the better. We need to devote an expiatory ceremony to Oromasis. How dreadful! He was to regenerate me in four days, and he is in this terrible state?'

'Let us eat, I say.'

'I'm afraid that the hour of Jupiter will soon be upon us.'

'You have nothing to fear.'

After the ceremony to Jupiter, I postponed the one for Oromasis to another day to draw up a great many cabalistic diagrams that the marquise translated into letters. The oracle said that the seven Salamanders had taken the real Querilinth to the Milky Way, and that the one who was presently in his bed on the ground floor was the evil Saint-Germain, whom a female gnome had put into this terrible state to bring about the death of Seramis, who was to perish of the same illness before reaching her term. The oracle said that Seramis should leave the task entirely up to Paralisée Galtinarde (me) and get rid of Saint-Germain, and to have no doubts as to the happy outcome of the regeneration, since the Word was to be sent to me by Querilinth himself from the Milky Way on the seventh night of my rite for the Moon. The last oracle proclaimed that I was to inoculate Seramis two days after the end of the ceremonies, after a charming water sprite had purified us in a bath in the very room we were in.

Having thus committed myself to regenerating the good Scramis, I thought of how I might avoid cutting a bad figure. The marquise was beautiful, but old. It was possible I might not succeed. At thirty-eight, I was beginning to find myself often subject to this misfortune of fate. The beautiful water sprite I was to obtain from the Moon was Marcolina, who, as my bath attendant, would instantly give me the regenerative strength I needed. I had no doubt of it. The reader will see how I had her descend from the heavens.

In a note, Mme. Audibert asked to see me before I went for supper with Marcolina. She joyfully informed me that Mlle. P.P. had received a letter from Genoa from Signor N.N., asking for his daughter's hand for his only son, whom she had met at Signor Paretti's, having been introduced by the Chevalier de Seingalt (me), who by now must have taken her back to Marseilles and returned her to her family.

'Mademoiselle P.P.,' Mme. Audibert told me, 'thinks he is most indebted to you as a loving father must be to someone who takes a paternal interest in his daughter. She herself has painted a most interesting portrait of you, and he insists on making your acquaintance. Tell me when you can come here for supper. His daughter will not be present.'

'That would give me great pleasure, for Mlle. P.P.'s husband will respect his wife all the more when he learns that I am a friend of her father. But I cannot come to supper. I will come any day you please at six o'clock, and stay with you until eight, and we shall meet before the husband arrives.'

I arranged this meeting for two days later and went to see Marcolina. I told her all the news, as well as how I would rid myself of my brother the following day; but I have already described this to the reader.

Two days later, as we were about to have dinner, the marquise smiled and showed me a long letter the rascal Passano had written her in terrible French which was nonetheless intelligible. He had filled eight pages to tell her I was tricking her, and to convince her of the truth of it, he told her the real story of the affair without hiding the slightest detail that might put me in the worst possible light. He also added that I had come to Marseilles with two girls I was keeping he knew not where, though he was certain I was sleeping with them every night.

Handing the letter back to the marquise, I asked her if she had had the patience to read it through, and she told me she had understood nothing, since he wrote like a savage. She had not tried to make sense of it, since he could only have written lies, to lead her astray at a moment when she most needed not to be deceived. Such prudence on her part pleased me a great deal, for it was essential to me that she not suspect the water sprite, the sight of whom would be indispensable to me if the mechanism of the flesh was to function.

After dining and running through all the ceremonies and oracles I needed to bolster the spirits of my poor marquise, I went to a banker to obtain a bill of exchange for one hundred louis drawn in Lyons to the order of M. Bono, and I sent it to him with a note instructing him that he should pay one hundred louis to Passano on the condition that he present my letter the same day as the date I had written on it. If he presented it after the day indicated, he was to be refused payment.

After taking care of this, I wrote the letter Passano was to present to Bono, in which I said to him:

Pay Signor Passano one hundred louis upon presentation of this letter, if it is presented to you on April 30, 1763. After this date my order becomes null and void.

With this letter in hand, I went into the traitor's room. He had been pierced in the groin by a lancet one hour before.

'You are a traitor,' I said to him. 'Mme. d'Urfé did not read the letter you wrote to her, but I did. Here are your choices, and you must make up your mind without protest, because I am in a hurry. Either you decide to be taken to the hospital today, since we do not want any sick people here, or you leave here in an hour and go straight to Lyons without stopping, since

I am granting you only the sixty hours that should suffice to travel forty stages. As soon as you arrive in Lyons, you must take this letter to M. Bono, who will pay you, on sight, one hundred louis, which I give you as a gift. After that you may do as you please, since you will no longer be in my employ. I make you a gift as well of the carriage, which was taken out of storage in Antibes, and shall now give you twenty-five louis for the journey. The choice is yours. But I warn you that if you choose the hospital I shall pay you only one month's wages, since I am dismissing you as of this moment.'

After thinking it over a little, he told me he would go to Lyons at the risk of his life, since he was very sick. Thereupon I called Clairmont to pack his trunk and told the innkeeper that Passano was leaving, so he would immediately send for post-horses. I then gave the letter addressed to Bono and the twenty-five louis to Clairmont to give to Passano as soon as he saw him get into the carriage, at the moment of departure. Once this was all taken care of, I went off to attend to my amorous pursuits. I was in need of some long conversations with Marcolina, with whom I seemed to be falling more deeply in love by the day. She told me daily that in order to feel completely happy she needed only a knowledge of French and a ray of a hope that I might take her to England with me.

I had never given her any reason to believe this would happen and felt sad at the thought that I would soon have to part with this voluptuous and obliging girl, born with an insatiable appetite for the pleasures of lovemaking and the table, where she ate as much as

94

I and drank even more. She was delighted that I had got rid of my brother and Passano, and begged me to accompany her sometimes to the theater, where all of high society approached her accommodating companion to find out who she was and scolded her when she would not let her reply. I promised to go with her sometime the following week.

'At the moment,' I told her, 'I am engaged in a matter of magic that takes up my entire day; but I shall need your assistance in it. I will make you a little costume in which to dress you up as a jockey, and in this attire you shall present yourself to the marquise, with whom I am staying, when I tell you, and hand her a note. Do you have the courage to do this?'

'Certainly. Will you be there?'

'Yes. She will speak to you, and since you do not speak French and therefore could not answer her, you shall pass for mute. The note will introduce you as such. The same note will say that you are offering your service to assist her at her bath, in my company. She will accept your offer, and when she tells you, you shall strip her naked, and then you shall do the same, and rub her from the tips of her toes to the tops of her thighs, and no further. While you are doing this in the bath with her, I shall strip myself naked, take the marquise in my arms, and for the moment you will merely watch us. When I separate myself from her, with your delicate hands you shall wash her private parts and then dry them. You shall perform the same function for me, and I shall couple with her a second time. After this second time, you shall wash her again, and then me, and you shall then cover with Florentine kisses the instrument with which I will have given her unequivocal signs of my affection. Then I shall take her a third time in my arms, and your role this time will be to caress us both until the end of the ordeal. You shall then give us a final ablution, and after having dried us, you will get dressed, take what she gives you, and return. I shall join you one hour later.'

'I shall do everything you ask of me, but you must know how difficult it will be for me.'

'No more than for me, because it will be you I shall be wanting to embrace, and not the old woman you will see before you.'

'Is she very old?'

'She will soon be seventy years old.'

'That old? I pity you, my poor Giacometto. Afterwards you will come sup and sleep with me?'

'Of course.'

'Very well, then.'

On the day appointed by Mme. Audibert, I met the father of my former niece, to whom I told the truth about everything, except that I had slept with her. He embraced me several times and repeatedly thanked me for having done more for her than he could have done himself. He told me he had received another letter from his correspondent, containing one from his son, which was submissive and respectful.

'He asked for nothing for her dowry,' he continued, 'but I gave him forty thousand ecus, and we shall celebrate the wedding here, for this is a very honorable marriage. The whole city of Marseilles knows Signor

N.N., and tomorrow I shall tell the whole story to my wife, who will forgive her daughter everything, thanks to this fine and happy event.'

I had to promise to come to the wedding with Mme. Audibert, who, because she knew me to be a great gambler and had held many games at her house, was surprised not to see me there. But I had come to Marseilles to create, not to destroy. Everything in its proper place.

I had a waist-length jacket of green velvet made for Marcolina, and breeches of the same material; I gave her green stockings, morocco leather shoes and gloves of the same color, and a green, Spanish-style snood that was long in the back and held her long black hair. Thus attired, she seemed a figure so worthy of admiration that had she shown herself on the streets of Marseilles, she would have been followed by all who set eyes on her, since she could not have been mistaken for anything other than a girl. Before supper I took her, in feminine attire, to my inn, to show her where she should hide in my room after the operation, on the day I was to carry it out.

As our ceremonies were completed on Saturday, I had the oracle set the time of Seramis's regeneration for Tuesday, at the hours of the Sun, Venus and Mercury, which, in the planetary system of magicians, follow one after the other as in the imaginary system of Ptolemy. These were to be the ninth, tenth and eleventh hours of that day, since, being Tuesday, the first hour belonged to Mars. The hours of the beginning of May were sixty-five minutes each; thus the reader, if he knows anything about magic, can see that I was to perform the operation on Mme. d'Urfé from half-past two until five minutes to six. On Monday at nightfall I took Mme. d'Urfé to the seashore, followed by Clairmont carrying a trunk weighing fifty pounds. Once I was certain no one could see us, I told Mme. d'Urfé the time had come and had Clairmont place the trunk at our feet and wait for us in the carriage. We then addressed a set prayer to Selenis and threw the trunk into the sea, to Mme. d'Urfé's great joy, which, however, was no greater than my own, since the trunk contained fifty pounds of lead. I had the other hidden in my room. Returning to the *Treize Cantons*, I left the marquise, promising to come back after I had given thanks to the Moon in the same place where I had performed my seven ceremonies.

I went to have supper with Marcolina, and while she was dressing up as a jockey, I wrote with rock alum on white paper, in capital letters; *I am mute, but not deaf. I have come from the Rhône to bathe you. The hour of Oromasis has begun.*

'Here is the note,' I told Marcolina, 'which you will give to the marquise when you appear before her.'

We left together on foot, entered my hotel unseen, and went into my room, where I hid her in a wardrobe. Then I put on a dressing gown and went to see the marquise, telling her that Selenis had set the regeneration for the following day at three o'clock; and it was to be terminated by half past five, to avoid the risk of encroaching on the hour of the Moon, which followed that of Mercury.

'You shall order the bath to be ready at the foot of your bed before dinner, madame, and make sure Brougnole does not enter your room before nightfall.

'I shall tell her to go for a walk; but Selenis promised us a water sprite.'

'That is true, but I haven't seen any.'

'Ask the oracle.'

'As you wish.'

She herself asked the question, renewing her prayers to the genius Paralis, requesting that the operation have the same effect if the water sprite failed to appear, since she was ready to bathe herself if necessary. The oracle answered that the orders of Oromasis were certain, and that she was wrong to doubt them. At this the marquise rose and performed a brief expiatory rite. This woman was incapable of inspiring pity in me, for she made me laugh too much. She embraced me, saying:

'Tomorrow, my dear Galtinarde, you shall be my husband and father. Ask the wise men to explain this enigma.'

I closed the door and released my water sprite from the wardrobe, who first undressed, then came into my bed, where she well understood that she needed to save me for the next day. We slept all night without looking at each other. In the morning, before calling Clairmont, I gave her breakfast and told her to go back into the wardrobe at the end of the operation, for she should not risk being seen leaving the inn dressed in this attire. I repeated the instructions to her, and recommended that she be cheerful and affectionate and remember

that she was mute but not deaf, and that at exactly half
past two she was to enter and present the note, on
bended knee, to the marquise.

Dinner was to be served at midday, and upon enter-
ing the marquise's room I saw the bathtub at the foot
of her bed, two-thirds full. The marquise was not there,
but two or three minutes later she emerged from her
dressing room wearing a great deal of rouge, a cap of
fine lace, a blond-lace mantelet that covered her bosom,
which forty years earlier had been the finest in France,
and an antique dress covered with gold and silver. She
wore emerald pendants on her ears and a necklace of
seven aquamarines supporting an emerald, as flawless
as they come; the chain holding it was of very white
diamonds, a carat and a half each, twenty-eight in
number. On her finger she wore a carbuncle I recognized, which she considered worth a million but I knew
was paste; but the other stones with which I was not
familiar were choice specimens, as I made certain
afterwards.

Seeing Seramis thus adorned, I felt I must flatter
her with my homage; and so I knelt before her and
tried to kiss her hand. She, however, would not suffer
this and invited me to embrace her. After she had told
Brougnole she was free until six o'clock, we discussed
our business until dinner was served.

Clairmont alone was allowed to serve us at table,
and on this day Madame wanted nothing but fish. At
half-past one, I ordered Clairmont to admit no one to
our chambers, and to go for a walk until six o'clock if
he so desired. Madame began to seem restless, and

I pretended to be a little so myself, glancing at my watches and again calculating the minutes of the planetary hours, saying only:

'We are still in the hour of Mars; the hour of the Sun has not yet begun.'

At last we heard the clock strike half-past two, and two or three minutes later the beautiful water sprite entered smiling, and with measured steps. She went directly to Seramis to deliver her note, with one knee to the ground. As the marquise saw that I did not rise, she herself remained seated but brought the genie to her feet, accepting the note, and was surprised to find it completely blank. I handed her a pen at once, and she understood she was to consult the oracle. She asked what the meaning of the note was. I took back her pen and made a pyramid of her question, which she interpreted to mean: *What is written in water can only be read in water.*

'Now I understand,' she said, and she got up, went to the tub, and plunged the note into it, reading in letters that were whiter than the paper: *I am mute but not deaf. I have come from the Rhône to bathe you. The hour of Oromasis has begun.*

'Then bathe me, divine genie,' Seramis said to her, laying the note on the table and sitting down on the bed.

Exactly as she had been instructed, Marcolina removed the marquise's stockings, then her dress, then her shift, and delicately placed her feet in the tub, and with the greatest speed stripped completely naked herself and got into the bath up to her knees. While

putting myself in the same state as they, I told the
genie to dry Seramis's feet, and to be the divine witness
to my union with her, to the glory of the immortal
Horosmadis, King of the Salamanders.

No sooner had my prayer been uttered than the
mute-but-not-deaf water sprite answered it, and I con-
sumed the marriage with Seramis while admiring
Marcolina's beauties, which I had never seen so well.

Seramis had once been beautiful, but she was as I
am today; without the water sprite, the operation would
have failed. Nonetheless the tender, loving, clean and
not at all distasteful Seramis did not displease me.
After the deed, I said to her:

'We must wait for the hour of Venus.'

The water sprite purified us in the places where the
aspersions of love could be seen; she embraced the
bride, bathed her to the tops of her thighs, caressed
her, kissing her from time to time, then did the same
for me. Enchanted with her good fortune, Seramis
admired the charms of this divine creature, inviting me
to do the same. I said I found her to be like no mortal
woman. Seramis became tender again, the hour of
Venus began and, encouraged by the water sprite, I
undertook the second assault, which was to be stronger,
for the hour had sixty-five minutes. I plunged into
battle, labored for half an hour groaning and sweating,
tiring Seramis without managing to reach the end, and
ashamed to deceive her. She wiped away the sweat that
mixed with powder and pomade as it poured from my
brow. The water sprite, who was caressing me more
and more provocatively, managed to preserve what the

old body I was obliged to touch destroyed, while nature denied the efficacy of the means I was using to come to the finish. Toward the end of the hour, I finally decided to bring matters to a conclusion, after feigning all the signs that normally appear at this tender moment. Emerging victorious from the struggle, and still menacing, I left no doubt in the marquise's mind as to my valor. She would have found Anael unjust had he told Venus I was a fake.

Marcolina herself was deceived. The third hour was beginning, and Mercury had to be satisfied. We spent one quarter of an hour immersed in the bath up to our loins. The water sprite enchanted Seramis with caresses of a sort entirely unknown to the Regent, the duke of Orléans. She thought them peculiar to river genies, and applauded the way in which the female genie worked on her with her fingers. Moved to gratitude, she begged the beautiful creature to lavish her treasures on me, whereupon Marcolina enacted all the teachings of the Venetian school. She suddenly became a Lesbian, and seeing me alive in turn, encouraged me to satisfy Mercury; but once again I found myself not without lightning, but without the power to explode in thunder. I saw the silent pain my efforts caused the water sprite, and noticed that Seramis herself wanted the struggle to end. I could go on no longer, and decided to trick her a second time with a death rattle accompanied by convulsions ending in stillness, the necessary conclusion to an agitation that Seramis, as she was to tell me later, found without match.

After pretending to have recovered my spirits, I entered

the bath, from which I emerged after a short ablution. As I began to dress myself, Marcolina did the same for the marquise, who looked at her with adoring eyes. Marcolina then dressed herself, and Seramis, inspired by her genie, took off the necklace and put it around the neck of the beautiful bath attendant who, after giving her Florentine kisses, ran away to shut herself in the wardrobe. Seramis asked the oracle if the operation had been perfect. Frightened by the question, I had it reply that the Word of the Sun was in her soul, and that she would give birth to herself with a changed sex at the beginning of February; but she must stay in bed for one hundred and seven hours.

Utterly content, she found divine wisdom in this order to rest for one hundred and seven hours. I embraced her, telling her I was going to sleep outside of town to gather the rest of the drugs I had left behind after the ceremonies I had performed to the Moon, and I promised to dine with her the next day.

I enjoyed myself infinitely with Marcolina until half past seven; since I did not want to be seen leaving the inn with her, I had to wait until nightfall to go out. I took off the fine wedding-coat I had on, put on a dress-coat, and accompanied her to her lodging in a hackney coach, taking with me the box of planetary offerings I had worked so hard to earn. We were both dying of hunger, but the elegant supper we were about to eat would ensure our return to the living. Marcolina took off her green jacket and put on a dress, after giving me the beautiful necklace.

'I will sell it, my dear, and give you the money.'

'How much could it be worth?'

'At least a thousand sequins. You shall go to Venice as the possessor of five thousand ducats; you shall find a husband and live with him in great comfort.'

'I will give you all five thousand ducats if you take me with you as your beloved mistress. I will love you as my very own soul: I shall never be jealous, and will take care of you as if you were my child.'

'We shall speak of that later, my pretty Marcolina. Now that we have had a good supper, let us go to bed, as I've never been so in love with you as now.'

'You must be tired.'

'I am, but not exhausted of my love, since – thank heavens – I was only able to distill myself once.'

'I thought twice. The good old woman! She is still attractive. Fifty years ago she must have been the greatest beauty in France. When we get old, we are no longer pleasing to Love.'

'What you caused to rise with such fire, she destroyed with a greater force still.'

'Do you always need a young girl in front of you when you want to be intimate with her?'

'Not at all, for the other times I shall not be required to engender a male child in her.'

'You were trying to make her pregnant? Ah, let me laugh, please. Do you think she believes she is pregnant?'

'Of course she does, since she is positive I gave her the seed.'

'How ridiculous! But why were you foolish enough to try three times?'

'I thought that with your presence it would be easy, and I was wrong. The flaccid skin I touched was not the same my eyes saw, and the culmination of my pleasure would not come. You shall see the truth of this tonight. Let's go to bed, I say.'

'Let's.'

By virtue of the comparison with the marquise, the night I spent with Marcolina equaled the nights I had spent with Henriette in Parma, and with M.M. at Murano. I stayed in bed for fourteen hours, of which four were devoted to love. I told Marcolina to dress appropriately and wait for me at theater time. She could not have been more pleased.

I found Mme. d'Urfé in bed, elegantly dressed, hair combed like a young woman's, and wearing a look of satisfaction I had never seen on her face before. She told me she owed all her happiness to me and proceeded to reason very sensibly in her madness.

'Marry me,' she said to me, 'and you shall be the guardian of my child, who will be your son too. In so doing you will keep my fortune in my own hands, and you will come into possession of what I shall inherit from M. de Pontcarré, my brother, who is old and will not live long. If you do not take care of me next February when I am reborn as a man, who will? God knows into whose hands I might fall! I shall be declared a bastard and lose an income of eighty thousand francs, which you could keep in my possession. Consider it carefully, Galtinarde. I already feel a man's soul inside me; I admit it, I am in love with the water sprite and I want to know if I may sleep with her fourteen or fifteen years from now. If such be the will of Oromasis, then it is possible. What a charming creature! Have you ever seen such a beautiful woman? It's a pity she is mute. She must have a male water sprite for a lover. But all water sprites are mute, since one cannot speak under water. I'm surprised she's not deaf. I'm surprised you did not touch her. Her skin is incredibly soft. Her saliva is sweet. Water sprites have a sign language one could learn. How happy it would make me to be able to converse with this creature! I beg you to consult the oracle and ask where I shall give birth; and if you cannot marry me, it seems to me I should sell everything I own to assure myself a future when I am reborn, for in my early childhood I shall know nothing, and will need money to give myself an education. If I sell everything, a large sum could be invested, which, in the right hands, would provide for all my needs on the interest alone.'

I replied that the oracle alone would be our guide, and that I would never allow her to be declared a bastard once she became a man and my son, and she seemed reassured on this account. Her reasoning was sound; but the argument was based on an absurdity, and I could only pity her. If the reader thinks that as an honest man it was my duty to set her straight, I protest: it was impossible, and even had I been able, I should not have done so, for this would have made her unhappy. By her very nature, the marquise could live only on chimeras.

I wore one of my finest coats to take Marcolina for the first time to the theater with me. Chance had it that the two Rangoni sisters, daughters of the Roman Consul, came to sit in the same box as ours. Since I already knew them from my first visit to Marseilles, I introduced Marcolina to them as my niece who spoke only Italian. It made Marcolina very happy at last to be able to speak to a Frenchwoman in her graceful Venetian tongue. The younger of the two, who was much more charming than the other sister, became Princess Gonzaga Solferino a few years later. The prince who married her, though poor, possessed literary talent and even genius, and was in any case of the Gonzaga family, being the son of the equally poor Leopoldo, and a Medini, the sister of the Medini who died in prison in London in 1787. Although Babet Rangoni was the poor daughter of the Roman Consul, she nonetheless deserved to be decorated with the title of a princess, for she had the airs and manners of one. And now she shines with the name of Rangoni among the lists of princes in all the almanacs. Her very vain husband is delighted that the readers of the almanac think his wife from the illustrious Modenese family of the same name. An innocent vanity. The same almanacs give the prince's mother, a Medini, the name of Medici. Such are the small falsehoods that issue from the pride of the nobility, which do society no harm. This prince, whom I saw in Venice eighteen years ago, was living on a sufficient pension given him by Empress Maria Theresa; I hope the late Emperor Joseph did not take it away from him, for he deserved it, both for his honorable conduct and his literary mind.

At the theater Marcolina spent the whole time chatting with the charming younger Rangoni, who wanted me to bring my companion to her house; I declined. I was thinking of a way to send Mme. d'Urfé to Lyons, since she was becoming a burden to me in Marseilles and I no longer knew what to do with her.

Then, on the third day after her regeneration, she had me ask Paralis where she was to prepare to die, which is to say to give birth, and I seized this occasion to have the oracle order that a ceremony should be performed to the water sprites on two rivers at once. This would resolve matters, for the same oracle also told me I must make three expiations to Saturn for the harsh treatment I had shown the false Querilinth. Seramis would have no reason to participate in this rite, since she needed to be present for the ceremony of the water sprites.

As I was pretending to think of a place where two rivers are close to each other, she herself told me that Lyons was watered by the Rhône and the Saône rivers, and that nothing could be easier than to do it in that city. I immediately agreed. Asking the oracle if there were preparations to be made, I had it answer that a bottle of sea water need only be poured into each river two weeks before the ceremony, a ritual of which Seramis could acquit herself in person in the first diurnal hour of the Moon each day.

'So we must fill the bottles here,' Seramis said, 'since all the other seaports in France are further away. I must leave as soon as I am able to quit my bed, and wait for you in Lyons. Since you must make expiations to Saturn here, you cannot come with me.'

I agreed, pretending to be sorry that I was forced to let her depart alone. The next day I brought her two bottles of salt water from the Mediterranean and instructed that she was to pour the bottles into the rivers on the fifteenth day of the current month of May. I promised to join her in Lyons before the two weeks had passed. We fixed her departure for the day after next, the eleventh. I gave her a written table of the hours of the Moon and the itinerary she should follow to spend the night in Avignon.

After her departure I went to stay with Marcolina. On that day I gave her four hundred and sixty gold louis which, together with the one hundred and forty she had won at *biribissi*, made her six hundred louis the richer.

[. . .]